Assessment Strategies for Online Learning

Issues in Distance Education
Series editor: Terry Anderson

Titles in the Series

Assessment Strategies for Online Learning

Engagement and Authenticity

Dianne Conrad and Jason Openo

AU PRESS

Copyright © 2018 Dianne Conrad and Jason Openo
Published by AU Press, Athabasca University
1200, 10011 – 109 Street, Edmonton, AB T5J 3S8

Cover and interior design by Sergiy Kozakov
Printed and bound in Canada

ISBN 978-1-77199-232-9 (pbk.)   ISBN 978-1-77199-233-6 (PDF)
ISBN 978-1-77199-234-3 (epub)   doi: 10.15215/aupress/9781771992329.01

Library and Archives Canada Cataloguing in Publication

Conrad, Dianne L. (Dianne Lynne), 1948-, author
     Assessment strategies for online learning : engagement and authenticity /
Dianne Conrad and Jason Openo.

(Issues in distance education series)
Includes bibliographical references and index.
Issued in print and electronic formats.

     1. Educational tests and measurements. 2. Distance education students.
I. Openo, Jason, 1973-, author II. Title. III. Series: Issues in distance
education series

LB3051.C66 2018   371.26   C2018-902629-4
                                         C2018-902630-8

We acknowledge the financial support of the Government of Canada through
the Canada Book Fund (CBF) for our publishing activities and the assistance
provided by the Government of Alberta through the Alberta Media Fund.

Canadä   Alberta
                Government

Contents

Foreword

Dianne Conrad and Jason Openo are problem-solvers. If one were to prioritize all the problems, challenges, and disagreements that have become fodder in debates within formal education, assessment would top the list for both teachers and for learners. Therefore, this is an important text, relevant to teaching and learning at any level, context, or use of technological support. Even more interestingly, the authors have focused their discussion on the special challenges and opportunities associated with online learning.

It has become popular to recite enrolment figures showing consistent global increases in the number of learners taking online courses; the number of institutions running and credentialing these courses; and the number of teachers struggling and gaining experience and skills to work effectively in this digital context. However, e-learning or online learning is but a subset of ways that education can be, and has been, distributed for the past 100 years. And, while they are distance educators, both Conrad and Openo have teaching experience that pre-dates the ascendancy of the Internet. This book brings forward their personal experience and insight, while presenting significant data gleaned from the extensive database of research literature both old and new.

This is clearly an innovative scholarly work. And though some readers may feel overwhelmed by the number of references and quotations sprinkled throughout the text, the book flows nicely from establishing a broad theoretical basis for online learning, through the asynchronous discussion-based learning model, to highlighting promising techniques and practices including group work, as well as self- and peer- assessment. The text also provides insightful glimpses of the assessment issues that have arisen alongside emergent forms of online learning including blended learning, the flipped classroom, MOOCs, wikis and badges.

Assessment is a dominant issue in higher education. In the 1990s, I recall being thrilled about the establishment of a research centre focused on student assessment at the large research university where I worked. I was however disappointed when I attended a few seminars and read papers from this group, as they had focused on creating valid multiple-choice exam questions using item analysis and statistical modelling that had little application to my own teaching of graduate students. Thankfully, this book is not *that* type of book! What you will find is theory, research, and very practical advice about the forms of higher education that are based on constructivist—with perhaps just a hint of connectivist—pedagogy. Constructivist teaching and learning pedagogy has evolved into a dominant form of education in the social sciences and humanities. Thus, don't expect tips on writing multiple-choice exams or learning analytics. However, you can expect very detailed discussions of the ways that learning can be assessed on individual and group levels, even as it is individually constructed in the minds and contexts of each learner.

There is much to recommend and a great deal of insightful knowledge in this text. It will appeal to practising teachers (even for those bound to classrooms); to professionals working as learning designers or developers to support teachers; and finally, to graduate students and online learning researchers. These latter two groups will no doubt use the text as a springboard to the many references and quotations that buttress and provide scholarly support to the ideas presented.

Finally, I'm thankful to the authors for publishing this text as an open access work. As the text highlights, we are entering an era of openness in scholarship. Since at least the 16th century, we have known of science and learning as a collaborative enterprise, which is best stated by Isaac Newton: "If I have seen further, it is by standing on the shoulders of giants." There are many intellectual titans in our universities today; however, many of their best ideas, experiments and insights are locked behind paywalls erected by commercial publishers. This is especially vexing as many practising teachers, even in affluent countries, do not have access to complete scholarly libraries, and those working in developing countries have almost no opportunity to, as it were, see further. This situation has changed and continues to evolve as more institutions, publishers, and authors embrace and benefit from open access to scholarly works. This text proudly takes its place (along with the dozen other titles) in the *Issues in Distance Education* series from Athabasca University Press. As series editor, I thank the authors for choosing to publish this work as an open resource. I also here commend Athabasca University for supporting the Press and the many reviewers and professional editors who have contributed to the work. As readers, you actually have an opportunity to thank these folks yourself, by ordering (and paying for) a hard copy or e-text— even after you have read it for free!

Terry Anderson, Professor Emeritus
Athabasca University

Preface

If we wish to discover the truth about an educational system, we just look into its assessment procedures. (Rowntree, 1977, p. 1)

Assessment. Evaluation. Grading. Do these terms equate simply to "judgment"? To success or non-success? For many learners, and also for many teachers and administrators, they do. But should they? We take the position that discussions of assessment or evaluation should not connect, on first principles, to the stringencies of judgment but rather to the potential of learning.

This is by no means a novel position. Learning theories have long embraced assessment as a central actor in the cycle of learning. However, the introduction and pervasive growth of distance education—specifically online learning or e-learning—in the last several decades has opened new doors for old questions about assessment: Why does learning require assessment? What kinds of assessment best honour and respect the learner? And the newer, distance-related questions: What kinds of assessment can measure learning activity that occurs at a distance? Can traditional forms of assessment continue to serve us well? (And its tacit corollary question: Did traditional forms of assessment *ever* serve us well?)

This book will not help you to construct a test or an exam. We will not elaborate on the affordances of technology or the intricacies of the hardware or software that support online learning. We do not discuss institutional assessment, or course or program evaluation; we deal only with the assessment of learning. Within that, we restrict our discussion to higher education, and, within that, we do not address the complexities of teaching and learning in the hard sciences.

The 2010 JISC Effective Assessment in a Digital Age report recently indicated that,

> despite potential benefits, adoption in higher education of the more complex opportunities made possible by technology is variable. Without departmental champions to support implementation, take-up of the more challenging aspects of e-assessment, especially in the context of summative assessment, has been slow. (p. 7)

In this volume, our objective is to discuss the assessment of online learning in higher education in meaningful and authentic ways. We are guided by constructivist philosophy and are concerned with the breadth and depth of assessment approaches, strategies, and techniques in the humanities and social sciences. While those who are engaged in more scientific fields may find useful material in these pages, we recognize that their areas of instruction employ, of necessity, alternative forms of assessment and evaluation.

Certainly, we hope that the material herein will be useful to teachers engaged in online teaching and learning, as well as those who would like to become involved in online teaching but are either hesitant or have not yet been given the opportunity. We feel that course designers and developers, as well as those involved in any way with curriculum, learning outcomes, or learning strategies, or those creating learning materials of any sort, will benefit from this read. We hope that graduate students interested in online learning and assessment or issues of quality, will find the book useful. Those who are engaged in online training in business and industry environments might also benefit. And, of course, we would like our colleagues and scholars in the field to explore these pages and make some use of them.

Structure and Organization

The book starts with a "big picture" framework that locates issues of assessment within the context of online learning, beginning with an overview of history, theory, definitions, and presenting a discussion of issues both underlying and concerning online assessment. There are many. We examine online learning's evolution from basic pedagogical principles, and we address questions of pedagogy and epistemology, of guiding philosophies, and of the nature of online learning so as to establish a framework for the assessment discussion. Assessment itself includes the logistics of what, when, why, and how, and of issues of authenticity and engagement. As it unfolds, the book narrows its focus to address specific aspects of assessment, including alternate forms of assessment arising from open learning, massive open online courses (MOOCs) and open educational resources (OER), blended and flexible learning, self-assessment, and social media's impact on assessment practice.

While we have tried to roll out a discussion on online assessment in a logical, sequential fashion, many concepts are inextricably interrelated. How can we tease out constructivism from a discussion of group work? How can learning outcomes be separated from course design? We have indicated as clearly as we can where to find various connected discussions within the book.

While it should be noted that this is *not* a book that will instruct readers on how to build tests or examinations, that this is *not* a guide to measurement—to questions of reliability, validity, or scoring—its pages nonetheless present many opportunities for immediate application to online learning environments, outlining strategies for appropriate evaluation planning and for creative and authentic assessments.

At the end of the book, we include an appendix entitled "Other Voices: Reflections from the Field" in which we share responses from colleagues on questions of assessment from their own practices. We hope that you find this supplementary material accessible and useful.

Assessment Strategies for Online Learning

1 | The Big Picture

A Framework for Assessment in Online Learning

Writing a book about assessment is tricky business for a number of reasons. Assessment has been described as "the heart of the student experience" and is "probably the single biggest influence on how students approach their learning" (Rust, O'Donovan, & Price, 2005, p. 231). Assessment is also highly emotional; students describe it as a process that evokes fear, anxiety, and stress (Vaughan, Cleveland-Innes, & Garrison, 2013, p. 81). It is fair to say that "nowhere are the stakes and student interest more focused than on assessment" (Campbell & Schwier, 2014, p. 360). A book on assessment goes to the heart of the complex dynamics of teaching and learning. As authors, we choose to wrangle with all the assumptions and ideologies of postsecondary education. Assessment in technologically mediated contexts adds another level of complexity to an already emotionally charged topic.

As such, a book on online assessment theory and practice, in particular, has never been more needed. In the annual Sloan Online Survey (Allen & Seaman, 2016), the proportion of chief academic leaders who report that online education is a critical component of their long-term strategy stood at 63.3% in 2015 (p. 5), with 2.8 million students taking all of their higher education instruction at a distance in the fall of 2014 (p. 10) and more than one in four students (28%) taking some of their courses at a distance, an all-time high in the United States. Distance courses "seem to have become a common part of the course delivery modality for many students" (p. 12). The growth of online education could see the migration of the worst aspects of traditional assessment into a new medium. Or, it could provide the opportunity to take an entirely fresh look, keeping the best of the traditional approaches while improving and innovating, supported by advances in technology.

Assessment is also connected to emerging perceptions of quality and the evolving nature of quality assurance processes within postsecondary education. Key trends in higher education have heightened focus on student assessment, especially in terms of online learning contexts, accountability, and the increasing scrutiny of the ability of colleges and universities to report performance outcomes (Newman, 2015).

Openo et al. (2017) contend that, at present, there is little connection between quality assurance indicators and quality teaching in provincial quality assurance frameworks, and that quality assurance reporting mechanisms are ill-defined. These gaps represent an important deficiency in provincial oversight of postsecondary education, where, increasingly, accreditation processes require detailed curriculum maps linking core competencies with assessment measures.

The need for robust quality assurance processes responds both to the still-lingering perception that online learning is ineffective or *not as effective* and the precipitous increase in online learning, which is becoming recognized as a crucial 21st-century skill, not just a mode of delivery. Online learning, according to Latchem (2014), "ceases to be mere delivery of digital learning products for the students' consumption and becomes a platform whereupon knowledge and learning are created by students through interaction, collaboration and inquiry" (p. 311).

The increasing demographic of adult learners (many of whom will study online) who want to gain competencies desired by employers has also led to a heightened awareness of the challenges and opportunities in assessment. A 2015 study from Colleges Ontario shows that 44% of current Canadian college students already possess postsecondary experience and return to college for the purposes of finding "that extra piece that makes them employable" or to "upgrade skills in a particular area" (Ginsberg, 2015, para. 4).

Any discussion of assessment must confront one of the great current debates in higher education. Educational goals once centred on individualization and personal development (what does it mean to be alive and human?), cultivating informed and active citizens, developing intrinsically valuable knowledge, and serving society through the public interest have narrowed. The perceived purpose of educational attainment has since narrowed to serving society through economic development. Wall, Hursh, and Rodgers (2014) define assessment as "a set of activities that seeks to gather systematic evidence to determine the worth and value of things in higher education" (p. 6), including the examination of student learning. They assert that assessment "serves an emerging market-focused university" (p. 6).

This narrower focus has led some to suggest that students "come into play only as potential bearers of skills producing economic value rather than as human beings in their own right" (Barnett & Coate, 2005, p. 24). Carnevale (2016) would both agree and disagree with this statement. He notes the irreconcilable ideas of democratic citizenship and markets, and yet he also recognizes that (like it or not) postsecondary education has become the United States and Canada's primary workforce development system. The focus on postsecondary education as a process of skills development to increase wages and one's social position leads to a double-edged sword. As "both a fountain of opportunity and a bastion of privilege" (Carnevale, 2016, p. 16), education becomes both equalizer and source of inequality. While we do not take a position on related issues of social justice and citizenship in this book, we do recognize that learning, assessment, and tangible outcomes are inextricably linked, and that "one of the most telling indicators of the quality of educational outcomes is the work students submit for assessment" (Gibbs, 2010, p. 7).

Assessment, then, provides evidence of the outcome in any outcomes-based approach to education. In Ontario, for example, "postsecondary learning outcomes are rapidly replacing credit hours as the preferred unit of measurement for learning," but "the expanded presence of learning outcomes at the postsecondary level has outstripped our abilities to validate those outcomes through assessment" (Deller, Brumwell, & MacFarlane, 2015, p. 2). Assessment practices are also increasingly focused on demonstrating acquisition of learning outcomes for the "purposes of accountability and quality measurement," because such measurement aligns with market-oriented aims, including closing the Canadian "skills gap," which causes Canada to lose as much as $24.3 billion dollars per year in economic activity (Bountrogianni, 2015). The perspective of students as potential bearers of skills to support economic development drives the move toward authentic assessment, where students can provide direct evidence of having meaningfully applied their learning (Goff et al., 2015). Using skills, knowledge, values, and attitudes they have learned in "the performance context of the intended discipline" (Goff et al., p. 13), learners simulate real-world problems in their discipline or profession. The purpose of this book is to support a move toward a new era of assessment and away from the current era, where "the field of educational assessment is currently divided and in disarray" (Hill & Barber, 2014, p. 24).

Aspects of Online Learning

The move to online learning in recent decades has raised questions about the nature of assessment with courses and programs. Is it the same? Is it different? How best to do it? This shift in assessment has moved like a glacier, slowly and yet with dramatic effect. The "traditional view of assessment defines its primary role as evaluating a student's comprehension of factual knowledge," whereas a more contemporary definition "sees assessment as activities designed primarily to foster student learning" (Webber, 2012, p. 202). Examples of learner-centred assessment activities include "multiple drafts of written work in which faculty provide constructive and progressive feedback, oral presentations by students, student evaluations of other's work, group and team projects that produce a joint product related to specified learning outcomes, and service learning assignments that require interactions with individuals, the community or business/industry" (Webber, 2012, p. 203). As Webber points out, there is a growing body of evidence from multiple disciplines (Dexter, 2007; Candela et. al., 2006; Gerdy, 2002) illustrating the benefits of learner-centred assessment, but these examples "do not provide convincing evidence that reform has actually occurred" (Webber, 2012, p. 203). The Appendix to this book includes examples from "reformers" who are gradually transforming the assessment landscape by innovating and incorporating new assessment approaches in online learning contexts.

We begin this discussion by first considering online learning, what it is, and how it serves learners. Now referred to as the fifth or sixth generation of distance education, online learning could be defined in terms of a spectrum of percentages (i.e., of time spent online). Some have defined it as learning done entirely online (Allen & Seaman, 2015), where most or all the content is delivered online with typically no face-to-face meetings. Others see online learning as an alternative access mode for the non-traditional and disenfranchised (Conrad, 2002), including both "busy professionals who travel extensively and unskilled labourers employed in jobs with inflexible hours that make a traditional school schedule unworkable" (Benson, 2002, p. 443). Some see online learning as a "new and improved" version of distance learning, where the affordances of online learning and the introduction of blended learning will surpass, in quality, what we have expected and accepted from the face-to-face classroom (Hiltz & Turoff, 2005). As Prinsloo (2017) observes: "We are trying to describe a very dynamic and fast-changing phenomenon, and the terminology often struggles to keep up with the reality of what's happening" (slide 41).

All of these definitions of online and blended learning can seem confusing or limiting, especially when "many distance education institutions, particularly the large-scale distance teaching universities, do not yet employ the electronic media as their main delivery medium, and most of the online education takes place at mainstream campus universities" (Guri-Rosenblit, 2014, p. 109). The questions of space and place become not just definitional but philosophical and ultimately pedagogical, as will be discussed in Chapter 3.

Among these many complex notions, a solid place to start a discussion of online learning and its affordances is at its technological ground zero, all the while keeping foremost in mind Salmon's adage: "Don't ask what the technology can do for you, rather [ask] what the pedagogy needs" (cited in JISC, 2010). What does the enhancement of learning by technology offer assessment practices? The 2010 JISC report names these eight advantages:

- Greater variety and authenticity in the design of assessments;
- Improved learner engagement, for example through interactive formative assessments with adaptive feedback;
- Choice in the timing and location of assessments;
- Capture of wider skills and attributes not easily assessed by other means, for example through simulations, e-portfolios and interactive games;
- Efficient submission, marking, moderation and data storage processes;
- Consistent, accurate results with opportunities to combine human and computer marking;
- Increased opportunities for learners to act on feedback, for example by reflection in e-portfolios;
- Innovative approaches based around use of creative media and online peer and self-assessment; Accurate, timely and accessible evidence on the effectiveness of curriculum design and delivery. (p. 9)

Online learning is also referred to, more or less synonymously, as e-learning. We will use the term *online learning* in this book and consider it a subset of the broader term *open and distributed learning* (ODL). The authors do not suggest that it is possible to offer a conclusive definition of "online learning," but we acknowledge key components of all offered definitions, such as the use of a personal computer or other mobile device connected to the World Wide Web using either a cable or wireless protocol, and the ability to make use of text-based, audio, and audio-visual communications that afford instructors the opportunity to create multifaceted and multidimensional instructional delivery systems. Or, as Dron (2014) has described it, "emerging systems" of instruction capable of being assembled and integrated "at a depth of sophistication that we have never seen before" (p. 260).

Online learning has exploded in recent years, as mentioned above. Once the purview of ODL single-mode institutions, online courses are now offered by most bi-modal and traditional higher education institutions. Online learning and ODL are subsets of the broader term "distance education," which itself was nurtured by tenets of adult education. (See Chapter 2 for this discussion.) Given this long developmental history, it is not surprising that the nature and shape of online learning has grown and benefited from the work of many theorists along the way. While it's not our intention to provide a comprehensive history of the field, a few major contributors should be acknowledged.

The foundational definition of distance education revolves around the separation of teacher from learner. "Separation" is most easily under-stood as a geographical separation, but in online learning, it can also be a separation in time. The term *asynchronous* refers to communication and interaction within online courses that occur at different times—times of the learners' and teachers' choice. In this work, we would like to turn away from the notion of "separation"—as it connotes some form of deficit—to one of "transcendence." When usefully applied, we maintain, technology can *transcend* the separation of space and time *as a limiting factor* due to the interactivity of Internet-based communications technology. Keegan (2005) has argued that teaching and learning is essentially composed of interaction and intersubjectivity where teacher and learner are united in a common purpoose.

Michael Moore famously addressed the notion of distance, which he referred to as independent study distance, in 1973 in what became the Theory of Transactional Distance. In it, he related studying at a distance to issues of structure, autonomy and control, and dialogue. His theory holds that a distance measured psychologically and physically between learner and teacher presents potential misunderstanding in communica-tion; therefore, that space needs to be minimized. The level of dialogue, the structure of the learning, and the degree of autonomy of learners are the factors that must work together to reduce transactional distance and ensure meaningful learning (Moore, 1993).

Even earlier, Charles Wedemeyer had outlined his vision for independ-ent study in higher education in 1981. He too saw potential for undue separation of teacher from learner in the name of choice and flexibility. His Theory of Independent Study gave more freedom to the learner while also placing more responsibility on the learner; but he also emphasized the need for good communication and a relationship between teacher and learner (Simonson et al., 2012, p. 43). In this, Wedemeyer is the predecessor to Anderson's observation that there is a tension between giving a student the full freedom of independent study and the instructional and learning benefits derived from participation in a learning community.

> Contrary to popular belief, the major motivation for enrolment in distance education is not physical access, but rather, *temporal freedom* to move through a course of studies at a pace of the student's choice. Participation in a community of learners almost inevitably places constraints on this independence, even when the pressure of synchronous connection is eliminated by use of asynchronous communications tools. The demands of a learning-centered context *might at times force us to modify the prescriptive participation in communities of learning, even though we might have evidence that such participation will further advance knowledge creation and attention.* (Anderson, 2004, para. 3, emphasis added)

In 1988, Otto Peters's Theory of Industrialization of Teaching looked into the future using theories of economics and industry to emphasize the need for mechanization, economies of scale, standardization, and careful planning and organization. Harsh as Peters's conceptualization of learning at a distance may sound, Saba (2014) outlines how Peters's thinking may have presaged the ongoing evolution of online learning, given the advent of new social media technologies:

> As personal technologies of communication, such as social media, became ubiquitous and faculty will be able to present mass personalized instruction to the learners with some level of standardization, it will be interesting to see how the dynamic between faculty and administrators change in the postmodern era.

From Sweden, Börje Holmberg introduced his Theory of Interaction and Communication in 1985. Although Moore (1993) categorized Holmberg's theory as a "smaller" theory than Peters's, it could be argued that interaction and communication is the more relevant theory in our discussion of teaching, learning, and assessment. Holmberg's seven assumptions underlying teaching and learning effectiveness include issues of emotional involvement, personal relationships, motivation, interaction, and this: "The effectiveness of teaching is demonstrated by students' learning of what has been taught" (Simonson et al., 2012, p. 48).

In 1995, Holmberg expanded his theory considerably, incorporating many aspects of distance education that had become characteristic of distance pedagogy; he wrote about "deep learning," about empathy, about "liberal" study and the benefits to society, and about the flexibility offered to a heterogeneous group of learners. He pronounced distance education an "instrument for recurrent and lifelong learning and for free access to learning opportunities and equity" (Simonson et al., p. 49). And while "free access" is, in many cases, wishful thinking, it is important to note here the parallel of adult educators, further discussed in Chapter 2 of this text.

Referring to Malcolm Knowles's Theory of Andragogy, Simonson et al. (2012) cemented the connection of distance education to adult education in this way: "Most now consider Knowles's work to be a theory of distance education; it is relevant because most often adults are involved in distance education, and andragogy deals with frameworks for programs designed for the adult learner" (p. 50).

To recap, then, pioneer distance educators stipulated conditions for which teaching and learning at a distance, with teacher separated from learners, could occur. Over the years and with advancements in Internet computer technology, online learning evolved as the preferred delivery mode. The capacity of Internet computer technology to provide online learners with deep and meaningful learning opportunities fostered a huge body of new literature that addressed technical affordances and pedagogy. While foundational theories contributing to online learning were well understood, deconstructing online learning itself has led mainly to discussions of teaching-learning theory and to the presentation of guidelines, strategies, models, and best practices. Online educators have no shortage of sources and materials to instruct them on "how" to engage with their learners. Learners have no shortage of resources to help them acclimate to the online medium or develop an online educational presence. Anderson (2008), in discussing the movement toward theory development, presented several models outlining the online process, but concluded that "the models presented . . . do not yet constitute a theory of online learning per se, but hopefully they will help us to deepen our understanding of this complex educational context" (p. 68).

From Technology to Interaction, Community, and Learner-Centred Pedagogy

Along the trail of developments in technology that both initiated and hallmarked online learning, there was an interest-shift from what *technology* could do to what *learners* could do, to how they would enable their learning through the technology available to them—in other words, a shift from a technology-orientation to a pedagogical orientation (Blanton, Moorman, & Trathan, 1998). We examine this shift here in terms of two central topics, which are not mutually exclusive: interaction and the Community of Inquiry (CoI). The related themes could be described as: (a) communication and its resultant interaction are key to online learning success; and (b) healthy learning communities engender appropriate and relevant levels of interaction.

Moore (1989), Wagner (1997), and Anderson and Garrison (1998) provided important early insights into the nature of interaction in computer-enhanced learning. Moore's initial categorization of three types of interaction—learner-learner, learner-content, and learner-instructor—was expanded into six possible types of interaction by Anderson and Garrison, who first broached the possibility of content interacting with content, foreshadowing semantic Web developments (1998). These discussions eventually included domains of interactions (cognitive, affective), frequencies of interaction, gender-specific interactions, and cultural-specific interactions (Conrad, 2009; Garrison, Anderson, & Archer, 2000; Jeong, 2007; McLoughlin & Oliver, 2000).

In 1998, Wenger's seminal work on communities of practice in the workplace laid the current foundation for the consideration of community-based interaction and communication. At about the same time, Garrison, Anderson, Archer, and Rourke's research on online presence (1998–2001) built on the concept of community and presented a new schema for understanding online learning in terms of cognitive, instructional, and social domains (Garrison, Anderson, & Archer, 2000). From that research evolved the equally important theory of CoI, defined as "a process of creating a deep and meaningful (collaborative-constructivist) learning experience through the development of three interdependent elements—social, cognitive and teaching presence" (CoI website). The CoI model has subsequently launched another stream of investigative research into the effects and relationships of its respective parts (Akyol & Garrison, 2008; Cleveland-Innis, Shea, & Swan, 2007).

A parallel and not-unrelated research stream was also dependent on Wenger (1998), Wilson, Ludwig-Hardman, Thornam, and Dunlap (2004), Stacey (1999), Bullen (1998) and Wegerif (1998), and some of the early work from Gundawardena and her colleagues (1995; 1997). It drew at the same time on adult education and learning theory literature to discuss community not as a learning laboratory per se but as an affective, social landscape. Tied most closely with Garrison, Anderson, and Archer's social presence literature (2000), this understanding of community focused on relationship-based interaction where "like-minded groups of people share[d] goals or special occasions" (Conrad, 2002). This understanding of community, taken from schools of social learning theory (Bandura, 1986; Vygotsky, 1978), moved the communication and interaction discourse closer to Garton, Haythornthwaite, and Wellman's (1997) prescient work on online social networking and also capitalized on adult learning theories from the works of adult educators K. Patricia Cross (1981), Dewey (1938), Knowles (1970), and Wlodkowski (1999).

The evolution from online learning's early technology-based curiosity to a more pedagogically based concern with learners and their learning has benefited from two recent theoretical centres—constructivism and blended learning. Building on those foundational pieces, scholars from around the world have contributed to our current understanding of online learning (Akyol & Garrison, 2008; Dron, 2007; Kirschner, Strijbos, & Kreijns, 2004; Mayes, 2006; Shih & Swan, 2005; Swan, 2002; Wilson et al., 2004).

The Community of Inquiry and Assessment

While it is not within the scope of this book to give CoI thorough and comprehensive coverage, we present it here as a very useful model of online learning and note that the CoI's approach to assessment very much falls in line with the spirit of a new era of assessment. Within the CoI framework, assessment is part of "teaching presence," the unifying force that "brings together the social and cognitive processes directed to personally meaningful and educationally worthwhile outcomes" (Vaughan, Garrison, & Cleveland-Innes, 2013, p. 12). Teaching presence consists of design, facilitation, and direction of a community of inquiry, and design includes assessment, along with organization and delivery. "Assessment very much shapes the quality of learning and the quality of teaching. In short, students do what is rewarded. For this reason, one must be sure to reward activities that encourage deep and meaningful approaches to learning" (Vaughan et al., 2013, p. 42).

Creating an Educational Experience

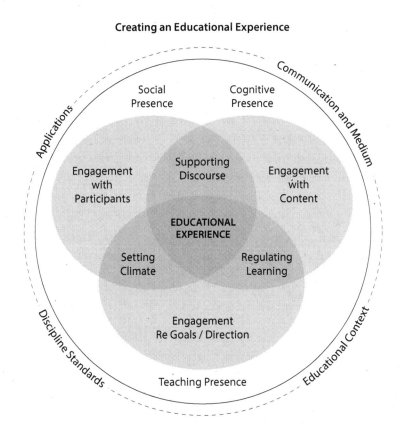

Figure 1.1. Creating an Educational Experience. The framework for a Community of Inquiry. Source: Garrison, R., Cleveland-Innes, M., & Vaughan, N. (n. d.).

In designing assessment through the CoI lens, it is essential to plan and design for the maximum amount of student feedback. "The research literature is clear that feedback is arguably the most important part in its potential to affect future learning and student achievement" (Rust et al., 2005, p. 234). Good feedback helps clarify what good performance is, facilitates self-assessment and reflection, encourages teacher and peer dialogue around learning, encourages positive motivational beliefs and self-esteem, provides opportunities to close the gap between current and desired performance, and can be used by instructors to help shape teaching (Vaughan et al., 2013).

Assessment and Evaluation

Assessment or evaluation? What is the difference between the two? First, it should be made clear that the two terms are often used interchangeably, perhaps due to carelessness, but perhaps also due to a lack of understanding of their respective meanings and the subsequent scope of application of each term. In her guide to assessment, Walvoord (2010) offers this definition: "Assessment is the systematic collection of information about student learning, using the time, knowledge, expertise, and resources available, in order to inform decisions that affect student learning" (p. 2). Similarly, in their text on evaluation, Fenwick and Parsons (2009) define evaluation as "the systematic collection and analysis of data needed to make decisions" (p. 3). The confusion begins here, with two definitions that are similar. We note also that Fenwick and Parsons point out that "evaluation" has long carried a negative connotation of being tested. We hold that this is one of the reasons that the gentler term "assessment" has become popular. Keeping in mind the constant intermingling of the two terms, we attempt here to pull them apart, beginning with Angelo and Cross's (1993) seminal work.

Angelo and Cross (1993) define assessment as an interactive process between students and teachers that informs teachers how well their students are learning what they are teaching. They continue, "the information is used by faculty to make changes in the learning environment, and is shared with students to assist them in improving their learning and study habits." (p. 427)

Angelo and Cross (1993) maintain that assessment is not grading. Evaluation, on the other hand, results in a grade being assigned to student performance—a performance that could include many aspects of studentship such as attendance, effort, or ability to exhibit good citizenship within the learning environment.

Adapted from Angelo and Cross (1993) and Neal (n.d.), Table 1.1 summarizes the key differences between assessment and evaluation:

Table 1.1. Key Differences Between Assessment and Evaluation.

Dimension of Difference	Assessment	Evaluation
Content: timing, primary purpose	*Formative:* ongoing, to improve learning	*Summative:* final, to gauge quality
Orientation: focus of measurement	*Process-oriented:* how learning is going	*Product-oriented:* what's been learned
Findings: uses thereof	*Diagnostic:* identify areas for improvement	*Judgmental:* arrive at an overall grade/score

Source: Angelo, T. & Cross, K.P. (1993).

Angelo and Cross's (1993) explanation, while sensible, has been challenged by others. The following table categorizes assessment in terms of two types, summative and formative. *Formative* is generally understood as interaction and feedback that is ongoing and that contributes to learning expertise, while *summative* occurs at critical and designated points in the learning process and is usually attached to a grade. The tension between assessment and evaluation is therefore apparent. Table 1.2 compares formative and summative assessment.

Given this seeming contradiction in terms, educators who speak of assessment are often referring to both assessment and evaluation when they speak of or use a blend of assessment strategies that are intended to improve learning and contribute to learner success as well as provide a means of measuring the observable product of that learning by issuing a grade. Angelo and Cross would say that we are not using the term *assessment* correctly. In the reverse sense, educators may not use the word *evaluation* correctly either. Nonetheless, this is often the semantic at play.

Table 1.2. Summative and Formative Assessment and Evaluation.

	Formative Assessment	Summative Assessment
Grading	Usually not graded	Usually graded
Purpose	Improvement: to give feedback to instructor and learners about how well learners understand specific material	Judgment: to derive a grade, and to allow learners to work intensively with course material
Focus	Very focused on whether learners have acquired specific skills or information	Less focused on specific skills or information; instead, allows learners to demonstrate a range of skills and knowledge
Effort	Requires little time from instructors or learners; simple; done in class	Requires more time from instructors and learners; complex; done outside of class

Note: Although we chose this document to illustrate, broadly, the differences between formative and summative assessment, it should be noted that there are many such typologies readily available from teaching and learning centres, universities, and individual authors.

Source: Center for Innovative Teaching and Learning (CITL). (2015).

Others have weighed in on this discussion in attempts to clarify the two terms. Noted educator Benjamin Bloom (1969) applied the same terms, formative and summative, to the task of measuring students' progress. In doing so, he suggested that "we see much more effective use of formative evaluation if it is separated from the grading process and used primarily as an aid to teaching" (Bloom, 1969, p. 48). What is critical here is that Bloom used the term "formative evaluation" while indicating that the same measurement tools could be used either formatively or summatively, depending on the intended use of their results. He agreed, however, that formative evaluation contributes to changes of something in some way. And while Wiliam (2006) states that "an assessment of a student is formative if it shapes that student's learning" (p. 284), he casts another light on the issue by suggesting that improvements in the development and use of formative assessment really constitute a professional development tool to assist teachers in enhancing their teaching performance.

Dunn and Mulvenon (2009) also attempt to explain the confusion: "Although an assessment may be designed and packaged as a formative or summative assessment, it is the actual methodology, data analysis, and use of the results that determine whether an assessment is formative or summative" (p. 2), again pointing to Bloom (1969), who complicated the differentiation between the two terms, in part by using the seemingly contradictory term *formative evaluation*. In what may be the most pragmatic and useful handling of the terms, Dunn and Mulvenon suggest that "formative or summative assessment data may be evaluated and used for formative or summative purposes" (2009, p. 3). In this text, we will generally use the term "assessment," but will stipulate "evaluation" when we are specifically referring to the assignment of grades.

Placed as a critical component with the learning cycle, therefore, assessment, defined as a mechanism for effecting changes in the learning process designed, ideally, for more productive performance, could be understood like this:

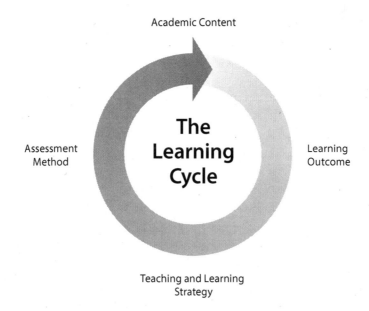

Figure 1.2. The Learning Cycle. Source: 2004 Teaching and Learning Services, McGill University.

As such, assessment is a core component of pedagogy and must be properly integrated into the learning cycle as a method of teaching that both reflects and contributes to learning. As a part of its contributory nature, assessment offers the opportunity to measure, in various fashions, the performance of both learners and teachers. However, harking back to the distinction drawn by Bloom (1969) and Cross and Angelo (1993), all too often the act of assessment is used instead to "audit" learning rather than "enhance learning and motivation" (Wlodkowski, 2008, p. 314); in other words, the process of assessing learners' progress in learning is regarded as evaluation. To further support his views on the notion of grades, citing comments by Milton, Pollio, and Eison in 1986, Wlodkowski continues:

> A grade is . . . a true salmagundi. Translated, this means a given grade can reflect the level of information, attitudes, procrastination, errors or misconceptions, cheating, and mixtures of all these plus other ingredients; all of this was noted in the literature over 50 years ago as well as today and is well known but ignored. The lone letter symbol is a conglomerate which specifies none of its contents. (pp. 352–353)

Dron (2007) analyzes grades (summative assessment or evaluation) and formative assessment in terms of control, outlining the negative capabilities of both. Of summative assessment, he concludes: "Whereas many aspects of control in education act more or less directly, the threat of summative assessment is latent and its effects are largely felt in the past, before it occurs" (p. 102).

From this misplaced faith in "the grade" flow a number of other academic transgressions, which include grade inflation, competitive actions among both learners and their teachers, performance review issues, and so on. Yet, both evaluation and assessment are a part of institutional life—indeed, ALL life—and will continue to be so. Given this, Wlodkowski suggests, "If we make assessments a partner and part of continuing learning and motivation . . . rather than merely audit by which to assign grades or scores, assessments themselves become important learning activities, worthy of everyone's time and effort" (2008, p. 329).

Concluding Thoughts

We have outlined, above, the concepts of both assessment-confusion and assessment-importance. We have presented an overview of distance education and online learning history that provides contemporary context, educationally, in what we term the "age of open," or, depending on where one stands on this philosophical divide, "the age of assault upon traditional education constructs."

Claims of change are rampant, aired in educational journals and at global conferences. Closer to home, Ontario's distance education network, Contact North, claims that "we are approaching an era in which new thinking about how we assess knowledge, competencies and skills start to bear fruit" (2016). This new era goes far beyond grades and includes badges, verified learning certificates, and micro-credentials, as well as prior learning assessment, designed to facilitate student mobility. In this new era, assessment will become a central component of any definition of quality. Within the Ontario Quality Assurance Framework, for example, "each academic unit is asked: What do you expect your students to be able to do, and to know, when they graduate with a specific degree? How are you assessing students to make sure that these educational goals have been achieved?" (Council of Ontario Universities, 2011, p. 12). Assessment flows directly from learning outcomes, and its importance in the educational transaction has grown. The strengthening focus on quality, accountability, and new opportunities demands a fresh look at assessment.

This book discusses assessment in a modern context where it is said that the "field of educational assessment is currently divided and in disarray" (Hill & Barber, 2014, p. 24). But this is not an entirely new claim. Over a decade ago, Barr and Tagg (1995) declared that a shift had occurred in higher education from an instruction paradigm to a learning paradigm and that learner-centred assessment was a central element in this new paradigm. Even though a growing body of literature exists that asserts that learner-centred assessment is a best practice in higher education pedagogy, Webber (2012) wonders whether faculty have fully embraced it, and her findings show little change in assessment practice from 1993 to 2004. Are we still shifting or have we arrived?

2 | The Contribution of Adult Education Principles to Online Learning and Assessment

It is often said—mostly by adult educators—that distance education is a child of adult education. That adage can be accepted in historical, geographical, and pedagogical senses. A short history lesson is in order so that the relationship of online learning and assessment principles to the larger domain of adult education is clear. We begin with definitions.

There are many definitions that purport to define adult education. Here are several, coined over the decades and the globe:

> All the deliberate methods by which men and women attempt to satisfy their thirst for knowledge, to equip themselves for their responsibilities as citizens and members of society or to find opportunities for self-expression. (1919, Report to the British Ministry of Reconstruction, cited in Selman & Dampier, 1991, p. 3).

> A process of public enlightenment and awakening regarding . . . the post war world. (Canadian Association of Adult Education, 1943)

> The entire body of organized educational processes, whatever the content, level or method, whether formal or otherwise, whether they prolong or replace initial education in schools, colleges, and universities as well as in apprenticeship, whereby persons regarded as adults by the society to which they belong develop their abilities, enrich their knowledge, improve their technical or professional qualifications, or turn them in a new direction and bring about

changes in their attitudes or behaviour in the two-fold perspective of full personal development and participation in balanced and independent social, economic, and cultural development. (UNESCO, in Darkenwald & Merriam, 1982, p. 9)

And from Eduard Lindeman, who professed in his writing that,

education is life—not a mere preparation for an unknown kind of future living. . . . The whole of life is learning; therefore, education can have no endings. This new venture is called adult education— not because it is confined to adults but because adulthood, maturity defines its *limits*. (1926, p. 6, emphasis added)

Although Darkenwald and Merriam (1982) claimed that any definition will be based on assumptions and value judgments that will not be acceptable to everyone, the broad intention of adult education can be clearly understood through these examples.

Likewise, the purposes of adult education—the "why?"—are many and varied. In his slim but useful book, *The Purpose of Adult Education*, Spencer (1998) elaborated on four purposes of adult education: vocational, social, recreational, and self-development. These basics were fleshed out by others. Jarvis (2010) identified these purposes:

- to maintain the social system and reproduce existing social relations,
- to transmit knowledge and reproduce culture,
- for individual advancement and selection,
- to provide for leisure time pursuit and institutional expansion, and
- to further development and liberation.

Well-known adult educators Darkenwald and Merriam (1982) presented their own list that included:

- cultivation of the intellect,
- individual self-actualization,
- personal and social development,
- social transformation, and
- organizational effectiveness.

Each definition and list of purposes outlines a field that is diverse and vast. Chapters in any adult education textbook will contain topics that address women and gender issues; citizenship; community; vocational enterprises and apprenticeship; labour unions; political and knowledge economies; work and learning; cultural and cross-cultural learning and teaching; social theory and practice; critical thinking and critical theory; environmental education; popular education and theatre; immigration and language; prior learning assessment and foreign credential recognition; literacy; social movements; professionalism; and of course distance education, online education, "open" education, m-learning, and MOOCs.

The history of adult education is diverse and rich (Selman, 2001; Selman, Cooke, M.Selman, & Dampier, 1998). Perhaps one of the first organized adult education efforts was the lyceums of the United States in the 1800s. Lyceum societies organized entertainment comprising speakers and debates the purpose of which was to foster social, intellectual, and moral growth in American. Chautauqua was another popular form of adult education in days gone by, where travelling tent shows presented "knowledge" and information of many sorts to the local attendees. The first Chautauqua was held in 1874 in Upper New York State; Chautauquas continued to travel the country with assortments of preachers, entertainers, magicians, speakers, and "teachers" until the early 20th century. Adult education became formalized through agricultural extension efforts when food production was an important way of life for America's early agriculture-based society; the University of Wisconsin was an early leader in that area.

In Canada, the University of Guelph assumed a prime "extension" role offering agricultural courses to Ontario farmers. Quickly becoming one of the largest providers in university extension by offering courses and learning opportunities at a distance as non-degree programming, the University of Alberta's Faculty of Extension, headed up by founding director Ned Corbett, expanded its reach across the province by means of travelling instructors, "magic lantern" shows, and, eventually, in 1933, the establishment of the Banff School of Fine Arts. Having now celebrated over 100 years of service to Albertans, the Faculty of Extension continues to offer courses that fulfill all adult education's roles listed above.

The education of adults, non-formally and outside the walls of formal institutions, had begun in Canada in 1606 in Port Royal (in what is now Nova Scotia) with the *Ordre de Bon Temps*, where gatherings of men "peer-educated" themselves with entertainment and discussion. Many other adult education enterprises flourished over the years; Canada's history is rich with world-renowned examples: the Antigonish Movement, Frontier College, the Women's Institute, the Mechanics' Institute, the YMCA (first formed in England to accommodate the crowds of young men migrating to the city from farm work during the Industrial Revolution), the National Farm Radio Forum (predecessor to the Canadian Broadcasting Corporation's show *Cross Country Checkup*), and John Grierson's National Film Board. The first adult education graduate degree program in Canada in adult education was introduced at the University of British Columbia in 1957.

After many years of active adult education activity affecting all sectors of society, adult education was recognized as a field. The Commission of Professors of Adult Education, a gathering of American adult education professors, was founded in 1959 to debate the theory and the principles underlying the practice. But already in 1943, the Canadian Association for Adult Education produced the following Manifesto, which outlined adult education's core beliefs.

———————◆———————

Manifesto of the Canadian Association for Adult Education (CAAE)

The Canadian Association for Adult Education confronting the challenge of world events, in its annual convention of May, 1943, desires to affirm its stand in regard to the basic issues of the crisis and to call upon all interested individuals and groups to share with the Association the urgent educational task of creating and strengthening those attitudes and understandings upon which a new Canadian and world society can be founded.

The C.A.A.E. believes that in this day of total war and total challenge, academic aloofness and neutrality are not enough and that it is obliged to declare itself categorically upon those basic issues of human principle which underlie the social and economic, and spiritual problems of our times.

The C.A.A.E. therefore affirms its adherence to the following principles:

(a) The principle of total and mutual responsibility—of each for all and all for each—both as between persons and as between nations. This must be made operative even towards the criminal or underprivileged individual and the guilty or underprivileged nation.

(b) Social controls and planning are a necessary expression of this sense of social responsibility. Planning need not necessarily involve governmental ownership of, control over, or active interference with, economic enterprises. Nevertheless, it is probable that the area of public ownership and control should be extended in those enterprises most essential to human welfare and where individual enterprise is unable or unwilling to operate in the public interest. It is still more desirable that the area of voluntary co-operative activity in every field should be increased.

(c) Human beings are ends not means. Planning must be combined with such local and community participation and democratic vigilance as to prevent the regimentation and frustration of the human personality. Social efficiency and social security are not ends in themselves but are for the sake of human dignity and personal fulfilment.

(d) Efficient service to the community—not social privilege, financial power, or property rights—should determine the status of the individual.

(e) The greater importance of consumption over production as the determining factor in economic activity must be re-asserted. Consumption goals, such as meeting decent standards of nutrition and housing, should be the main incentive of economic life.

(f) Social goals take precedence over individual and sectional purposes of profit or advantage. This principle asserts itself in time of war and must be maintained for the winning of the peace. Great collective purposes of social security, world nutrition, slum clearance, reforestation, soil conservation etc., are emphatically necessary as binding forces uniting our people, motivating economic life, and giving dynamic content to planning and to the effort after full employment.

(g) Neither the old individualism nor the newer mass-collectivism but a relationship of voluntary co-operation, which balances rights with responsibilities, is the basic pattern of the emergent social order. Such a relationship of voluntary co-operation has a place for central planning and control as well as for the legitimate liberties and enterprises of the individual. In the international sphere it supports the obligations of a collective system for defence and for the maintenance of world peace.

The C.A.A.E. will seek the co-operation of all individuals and organisations who endorse these principles in formulating and executing a whole-hearted campaign of public education directed towards the winning of a people's war and a people's peace.

Please hang this up for ready reference.

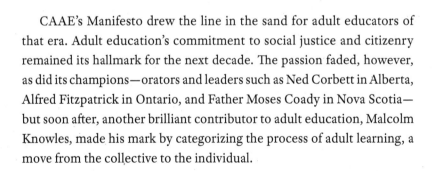

CAAE's Manifesto drew the line in the sand for adult educators of that era. Adult education's commitment to social justice and citizenry remained its hallmark for the next decade. The passion faded, however, as did its champions—orators and leaders such as Ned Corbett in Alberta, Alfred Fitzpatrick in Ontario, and Father Moses Coady in Nova Scotia— but soon after, another brilliant contributor to adult education, Malcolm Knowles, made his mark by categorizing the process of adult learning, a move from the collective to the individual.

Assumptions Underlying Adult Education

In 1970, Malcolm Knowles, often regarded as one of adult education's "fathers," outlined four basic assumptions of adult education upon which he built his andragogical stance. Knowles's assumptions have become the basis for modern adult education study, although more recent critical theorists have questioned the wisdom of placing such heavy emphasis on the state of the adult learner rather than on the role of adult education in creating a more just society. Knowles's four assumptions are:

- Recognizing the concept of the learner as moving from dependency toward self-direction, although at different rates and in different ways

- Valuing learners' prior and experiential learning and the corresponding value of "active" learning

- Recognizing that adults learn when they are ready to learn and that learning occasions should capture adults' sense of readiness and eagerness in order to fulfill their need for social competency

- Recognizing that adults' competency-orientation results in a new time perspective that values immediate application rather than a subject-centred postponed application

From these assumptions, the rationale underlying distance education is discernible. Knowles described adults as independent learners, who are ready to take control of their own lives through educational experiences, who will draw on their own past experiences to build new knowledge, and who are ready to learn now. As we focus here on higher education, Knowles's work provides the foundational knowledge for examining adult learning and its offspring, distance learning.

If this sounds like a prescription for the take-up of distance education—for motivated learners to seize opportunities to learn that fit their lifestyles and their schedules—it is. The first generation of distance education delivery was correspondence, a "course-in-a-box." If one accepts the history of distance education as divided into five generations, then that history looks like this:

- First generation: correspondence education

- Second generation: "integrated use of multiple, one-way media such as print and broadcast or recorded media such as video-cassettes"

- Third generation: "two-way synchronous tele-learning using audio or video-conferencing"

- Fourth generation: "flexible learning based on asynchronous online learning combined with interactive media"

- Fifth generation: "intelligent flexible learning, which adds a high degree of automation and student control to asynchronous online learning and interactive multimedia." (Bates, 2008, citing Taylor, 1999, p. 217)[1]

As Spencer (2004) pointed out, the issues that define distance education are the issues of adult education:

> Distance education (DE) is essentially a delivery method, and most of the more challenging issues in DE are issues to be found also in education generally and in adult education in particular. For example, questions of access, equity and pedagogy, and the overarching questions as to the purposes of adult learning (for economy, transformation/social change, diversity etc.), are generic to education. The DE perspective adds a twist to these issues: it flavours them without substantially changing their essence. (p. 189)

Distance education and online learning have evolved since Spencer wrote this in 2004; it could be argued today that there has *indeed* been a change in "essence," largely driven by an explosion in social media that we could not (or did not) foresee at the time. However, correctly so, he cautioned that distance education—and online modes—provides delivery vehicles for adult-styled learning, as defined by Knowles's assumptions.

---

1 There is disagreement among scholars on the number and classification of generations. Some argue that distance education is currently in its sixth generation, approaching a seventh. The sixth generation is described as based on Web 2.0 and features an increased use of social software tools such as blogs, wikis, and YouTube that enhance learning opportunities (White et al., 2015, p. 104).

The missing ingredient in the mix that constitutes today's online learning capabilities was technology, and, as evidenced above through the generations, developments in technology fostered corresponding growth in distance education's ability to enhance delivery modes and, ultimately, serve more learners in more diverse ways.

This correlation by no means implies that adult education *drove* distance education. There are many factors in distance education's rise to its current heights, among them the aforesaid advances in technology, globalization and a shrinking world, and also the American military's concern with making more education available to its members (Kasworm, 2010). The University of Maryland's University College still caters to a large number of American servicemen overseas and their mandate is reflected in the ongoing popularity of their distance programs.

However, as Spencer (2004) points out, self-directed, lifelong, accessible education—hallmarks of distance education—are fundamental tenets of adult education. And while earlier generations of distance education, specifically correspondence education, offered limited opportunity for the types of shared and collaborative learning prized by adult educators, well-designed online learning invites participation, collaboration, and critical discourse. The ways in which online learning offers these opportunities are discussed at more length in Chapters 4 and 7.

Spencer supports this contention with research from Deakin University in Australia, where researchers' critical perspectives on distance education confirmed its harmony with liberal adult education (Evans & Nation, 1989; Evans & King, 1991). As we have done in this text, the Australian scholars "locate [their consideration of distance education] within the subject areas of education and social science" (Spencer, 2004, p. 195) and highlight cases of learner-centred course design that offers "more student choice, more open-ended projects, experientially based assignments and interactive materials" (2004, p. 195).

The Australian research is old research, and the sixth (or seventh) generation of distance education, now almost solely conducted online, is further advanced in its use of collaborative tools than was the case when Spencer contemplated 2004's distance education status. That said, the relationship between distance education and adult education was observed in the very foundational aspects of distance education's raison d'être: increased access and opportunity for adult learners and the encouragement for motivation and self-direction, both of which imply maturity and the acceptance of adult education theory.

Online Learning and Adult Learners

Today's online learning affordances magnify and enhance the spirit of adult education theory. And while we realize that online learning extends its reach to many other demographics, we focus here on higher education. Within adult education, there is nuance in the definition of adulthood. Age is understood to be an inadequate defining parameter, as the various ages for being considered "adult" differ geographically and politically, even within one jurisdiction, such as Canada. The best way to define adult is by psychosocial means, which refers to an individual's ability to meet the responsibilities usually conferred upon adults by the society in which he or she lives.

The literature, some of it reviewed and cited above, tells us with certainty that adults have a preferred style of learning. By "learning style" here, we are not referring to the more scientific breakdowns of Kolb, or even to the distinctions between visual, auditory, or kinaesthetic learning—although research shows that most adults combine these modes and, overall, prefer the kinaesthetic approach (MacKeracher, 2004). Knowles's (1970) work also provides us with a good sense of how adults like to learn.

Adults Learning in Their Own Way

Simply removing adults from a traditional classroom, with its overtones of "school days," helps adults feel less like children and more like themselves. Even in traditional face-to-face classrooms, adult educators work to ensure that adults are not treated or made to feel like children. There are strategies to accomplish this: Do not place adults in little desks; do not arrange the desks in rows; try not to have adults looking at the backs of others' heads; do not "lecture" to adults; do not turn your back and write on a blackboard (blackboards are generally out of style now, but even whiteboards can offend); manage a flexible classroom with appropriate occasions for movement (adults get sore); do not read from PowerPoint slides (adults can read); and so forth. Peter Renner's excellent guide to teaching adults provides useful tips and hints in this regard, while Brookfield's classic *The Skillful Teacher* offers more research-based and theoretical advice (Brookfield, 1990a; Renner, 1993).

As a part of adults' need for respect is an appreciation of fairness. Fairness is a slippery concept, but adults recognize it when they see it and more so when they don't see it. In his blog, Downes (2010) makes an impassioned plea for fairness as a societal necessity, while acknowledging at the same time the difficulty with defining or implementing it. Complicating the issue further is the acknowledgement that *fairness and equality are not the same thing.* As Butler states (2004, p. 105), "What is fair for one student may not be fair for another." Butler goes on to critique the notion of fairness "simply as a technical affair with test construction" (p. 105). It is more than that, larger than that. Fairness includes not just the product by which learners are assessed but the context that precedes assessment and the outcomes of that assessment. What consequences to learners follow from assessment?

Put another way, the authors cited above are calling for authentic assessment that aligns with learning activities framed within the learning cycle. They are calling for assessment that makes sense to learners because it reflects the collaborative knowledge of the group, constructed on adult principles. Assessment, in these cases, is fulfilling its role as best it can, for both learners and teachers.

Online learning can address these adult preferences. Learning online can allow adults to create the ambience that suits them and fosters optimal conditions. With autonomy, however, comes responsibility (Garrison & Archer, 2000); we assume adults have reached the level of maturity whereby they can manage their autonomy successfully. One of the issues with online learning among younger learners, for example, high school youth, is the lack of maturity that is often demonstrated through behaviours and absences (Palahicky, 2017).

Flexibility and Choice for Adult Learners

It's safe to say that the largest advantage to online learning is the flexibility it offers learners—including "open" learning. Open learning can be defined in a number of ways (see Chapter 6 for this discussion), and online learning is not necessarily open. But it *is* flexible, available in both synchronous and asynchronous formats. The asynchronous format does not require attendance or performance in real time. Synchronous delivery, on the other hand, does set a time for an online learning group to show up for real-time exchange. Though this is generally not favoured as much by learners for obvious reasons of convenience or inconvenience, synchronous sessions can still add substance to an online environment. In most cases now, synchronous sessions are recorded for flexible access at a time of the learners' choice.

Online learning permits choice in other ways as well, both curricular and logistically. To explain this, we consider course design and the pragmatics of engaging learners at a distance. Consider, by comparison, the dynamics of a face-to-face classroom where the person at the front of the room launches a topic or question to the group and all attention focuses on that particular topic. The physics of one-place, one-time creates a cognition-cluster around that issue, and it can be dealt with in a prescribed amount of time. As this is not possible online, given its usually asynchronous nature, good online design calls for a variety of stimuli, possibly questions, possibly other avenues for participation, so that the dissemination of focus and time still keep learners engaged through diversity and choice. This strategy can be likened to small group activity within a classroom where different groups are tackling different topics. More conceptual ground is covered, learners can enjoy the opportunity for diversity, and it's possible to have made the choice of topic open to them.

Garrison and Archer (2000) discuss another aspect of the "worthwhileness" (p. 163) of choice. They acknowledge, quite practically, that it is not possible to cover every aspect of a particular topic. Given that constraint, "decisions have to be made as to what is essential for understanding if students are to have the time to approach their learning in a meaningful manner" (p. 163). This consideration highlights both choice and authenticity. Within well-designed curriculum, learners may be given a choice of "topic-within-topic," whereby they can choose among approaches or perspectives on a certain topic, and bring their individuality or experiential learning to the topic. Garrison and Archer (2000) point out that "if students are to accept responsibility for their learning, then choice, negotiation, and agreement must be part of the process. This process is dependent upon a responsible and collaborative process of assessing students' current goals, motivation and knowledge" (p. 148).

The adoption of the constructivist approach to learning plays into online design here. In believing, as constructivists do, that learners will engage in knowledge-creation as a group, each bringing the value of his or her own experiential learning to the table, the offering of topic choice to learners opens up the possibility of "fit," of relevance of the topic at hand to learners' experiential history. Topic A doesn't ring a bell? Try Topic B. The canny designer chooses an array of topics that reflects the theme or content at hand but also provides a number of different entry points to the discussion, with something for everyone.

Connection and Purpose among Adult Learners

These adult needs are consonant with the notion of choice. Adults choose to learn when they feel they need to (Knowles, 1970); from their choices there should arise a sense of purpose, since they have acted upon either intrinsic or extrinsic motivators (usually a combination of both) and thereby moved toward their goal.

The issue of "connection" in online learning occupies a lot of literature in our field. It should not be contentious, as there is sound empirical data that illustrates the value of social affinity and connection among online learners (Conrad, 2014; Conrad, 2005; Ross, Gallagher, & Macleod, 2013; Shackelford & Maxwell, 2012). However, some learners, especially novice learners, equate sociability with visual presence, and, except for occasional webcam use, it is obviously not possible to see fellow learners at a distance. That said, the literature referred to above shows that a great deal of social activity and a strong *sense* of sociability can be established and can exist online. Dewey, Garrison, and Archer (2000) maintain "the coordination of the social and psychological factors to be the ultimate challenges for the educator" (p. 14). The social aspect of online learning is called community, and building community involves careful and strategic work by designers and instructors (Conrad, 2005; Rovai, 2002). It involves trust, safety, humour, and social presence, as described in Chapter 7.

Most adults value online community and the relationships that emerge from well-constructed and facilitated courses that permit and encourage social connection. Not all do, however. Again, learners choose the level of sociability that they wish to bring to the course. Interestingly, gender researchers often attempt to illustrate that women are more socially active online than are men. We are not aware of any reports that successfully establish that this is so.

Adults Learners: What They Need to Learn

Two of Knowles's (1970) precepts involve adult learners learning material that they feel they need to learn in order to problem-solve or to address a concern—for example, the need to improve a set of skills or obtain a credential in order to advance at work. One of the ways that adults make sense of learning material is by scaffolding that material to previous knowledge or to some aspect of their learning history. Essentially, what this means is that adults need to be given the opportunity to talk about themselves, their workplaces, their experiences, and their reflections and need to be given the chance to bring their experiential knowledge, from wherever it was gleaned, to the learning at hand.

A Cautionary Word Concerning Constructivism and Autonomy

Even as constructivists advocating for adult learning principles in technology-supported online learning environments, we recognize some level of constriction of approach. To those who say, "This type of learning is not possible for me in my practice," we offer these caveats and the following research.

We begin with the often misunderstood notion of self-direction in adult learning, which does not imply "free rein" for learners in their learning. Rather, self-direction refers to learners' active and responsible involvement in choosing their learning paths, setting goals, and self-monitoring their progress and motivation along the way (Candy, 1991; Garrison & Archer, 2000; MacKeracher, 2004). Learners do not cede the need for guidance, and educators should not abnegate their responsibility to "teach," which Brookfield (1990a) considers a moral obligation. Facilitating adult learning in a learning-centred environment does not imply or permit a lack of presence, but rather the recognition that "delivering" education in the method termed "banking" by Freire (1970) is not a preferred way of learning for adults. The understanding of facilitation skills in adult education is based on Rogerian concepts that prize autonomy, empathy, and the exercising of a "sensitive awareness of the way the process of education and learning seems to the student" (Rogers, 1969, p. 111).

The teacher-as-facilitator, then, is present and responsible for adhering to the curriculum in such a way that learning outcomes are met. In our constructivist design, adult learning principles will be met also; the learner actively engages in collaborative knowledge building and exercises some degree of choice within the range of topics. How much autonomy, though, is enough? How much interaction, how much collaboration, how much content-presentation—and in which ways? As Garrison and Archer (2000) point out, many of these pedagogical issues can be negotiated within the group, assuming that adult education principles are introduced, explained, and understood. (Further discussion on group issues and assessment is found in Chapter 5.)

Here, however, we present an example from a hypothetical history class that illustrates the theory presented in this chapter. The Stanford History Education Group (n.d.) points out that memorizing and recalling historical facts is an old approach to learning history, not reflective of the constructivist philosophy. They also state that "constructivism is not a prescription for how to teach" and acknowledge that the discovery method of searching out solutions is not universally useful nor applicable. This realization echoes a current argument in the teaching of children's math, where a backlash against discovery-math approaches seems to indicate that some things are just better accepted as fact, while leaving the excitement of "discovery" to more complex, problem-centred issues.

In order to demonstrate the complexity of history and the importance of interpretation, students might be assigned to projects that require them, armed with facts, to create their own analysis or interpretation of those data. Not only does the flexibility of online technology make project work accessible over time and space, but technology's affordances enable archival research and connectivity to, and interaction with, global resources.

Concluding Thoughts

This chapter outlined adult education's relationship to online learning, specifically in a foundational role; it serves to preface the following discussion, which continues to relate adult education principles to online learning—this time with a focus on assessment. Online learning is seen here as the "offspring" of adult education, reflecting adult education's concepts and principles, and carrying forward its respect for adult learners' learning preferences and characteristics.

3 | What Do You Believe?

The Importance of Beliefs about Teaching and Learning in Online Assessment

The chapter title above uses the word "beliefs" rather than "philosophy," which is what this chapter is *really* about. While not synonymous, these words are inextricably related, and, regardless of the term you are comfortable with using, the bottom line is that successful teaching and assessment requires you to be aware of your own approach to teaching, learning, *and* assessment. In their 2009 text on evaluation, Fenwick and Parsons stipulated:

> To bring your evaluation and teaching practices into line with your ideas, you need to reassess your philosophy of teaching and ask yourself if your methods and criteria for evaluation match your beliefs about what and how adults should learn. (p. 13)

Following this declaration, Fenwick and Parsons (2009) presented four stories illustrating the contexts and results of occasions when teachers' philosophies of teaching, learning, and assessment did not align with their actions. The unfortunate outcomes—all from different courses and classes—ranged from students' cynicism, to accusations of fraud, to complaints to the department chair.

How do we know what we believe in? How do we identify our teaching philosophy? What do we believe about how learners learn? Theorists and educational philosophers have identified schools of belief—different approaches to teaching and learning—and various theorists have created typologies, or categories, of philosophies. Before examining some of these typologies, it's useful to review our own views of instructional practice. Fenwick and Parsons suggest asking yourself these questions:

- What are the most important things that learners should know or do by program's end?
- Is knowledge created by learners or should they master the knowledge given to them by others?
- Which is more important: collaborative learning or individual learning?
- Who should control learning, the instructor or the learner?
- Is learning systematic and sequential, or is it holistic and idiosyncratic?
- Do we grasp learning—"aha!"—or grow into it?
- Can learners be viably asked to demonstrate their learning immediately after the learning experience or should they be given time to reflect? (2009, p. 15)

The potential answers to these questions indicate the different ways that one can approach these aspects of learning.

Overview of Philosophical Orientations to Teaching and Learning

Of the several typologies available to distinguish among philosophical orientations to teaching and learning, the one that follows here is perhaps the most popular, having been presented by Darkenwald and Merriam (1982), Zinn (1990), Draper (1991), and Lange (2006).[2] This classification outlines five philosophies that may underpin and guide our teaching.

---

2 For a fuller list of typologies over five decades of Canadian and American thought, see MacKeracher 2004, pp. 17–18. We use the term *philosophical orientations* to refer to various sets of beliefs on which educational practice is founded. One also

Liberalism

Liberalism is considered the oldest philosophy of teaching, harking back to the classical period. Socrates, Plato, and Aristotle extolled the virtues of the human mind, arguing that rational thought would lead us to truth. Learning was for learning's sake—for the sake of acquiring wisdom, as opposed to practical skills. From the liberal philosophy came "liberal education" and the liberal arts college. Lange (2006) writes that liberalism is based on the maxim that "knowledge sets you free" (p. 96). A liberal arts education includes subjects in both the humanities and social sciences (fine art, literature, history, political theory, sociology, anthropology, language studies, and so on). What is important to note for our purposes regarding assessment is that the liberal philosophy privileges the expertise of the teacher over the knowledge held by students.

Progressivism

The progressive philosophy sprang most immediately from 19th-century scientific advancements and from ideas about social progress that developed out of Darwin's theory of evolution. Scientific and technological discoveries encouraged the belief that all things were possible, following the principles of experimentation, logic, and problem-solving. As Lange (2006) notes, the progressive approach to education can be traced back to Jean-Jacques Rousseau, with his faith that human beings were "born with unlimited potential for growth in a nurturing environment" (p. 97) and that education should allow children's natural curiosity to flourish. Progressivism thus differed from liberalism in its emphasis on science, empirical forms of learning, and the practical dimensions of knowledge. The American pragmatist John Dewey contributed to progressive thought, holding that "scientific and social literacy were necessary components of a strong democracy of thoughtful, responsible citizens" (Lange, 2006, p. 97). Education was perceived as the future; its application promised an answer to society's problems.

---

encounters the terms *philosophies, approaches,* and *paradigms,* all with reference to the same thing.

Behaviourism

Nineteenth-century industrialization and its resultant technological focus gave rise to the notion that the environment—and human behaviour— could be shaped, controlled, and measured using systems of reward and punishment. B.F. Skinner's study of classical and operant conditioning, using rats, pigeons, and dogs, focused on stimulus and response in order to evoke desired behavioural changes. In education, behaviourism found favour in vocational and technical training, where learning was observable and measurable. Behaviourist adult education espoused behavioural objectives that directed sequenced content and favoured learning.

Humanism

Exactly contrary to behaviourism, humanism aspires to foster and develop individuals' potential for self-actualization through recognizing their autonomy, freedom, and dignity. Humanism's belief in inherent human goodness dictated that individuals would strive to better themselves and their world. Based on the humanist psychology of Carl Rogers and Abraham Maslow, humanism prizes student-centred learning environments and casts the teacher's role as one of facilitation and support, helping learners on their educational journey with positive support and the freedom to choose. Humanism embraces Knowles's (1970) assumptions and values reflection, self-direction, and personal knowledge.

Radicalism

Radicalism pushed humanism to its extreme; individuals could only reach their full potential when not oppressed or limited by society. Using Freire's (1970) *conscientization* as a founding principle, radical thinkers see society as flawed by social injustice and power imbalance, thus creating conditions of marginalization for many of society's groups such as women; immigrants; gays, lesbians, and the transgendered; the poor; the illiterate, and the challenged or disabled. Education is seen as a tool for those in power, and, through a "process of empowerment, marginalized peoples can collectively uncover the power relations and hegemonic ideologies" (Lange, 2006, p. 201) that oppress them and keep them contained and unable to realize their true potential. This is a philosophy sensitive to power; this is a philosophy that demands action.

The "big five" schools of thought, outlined above, have been supplemented over the years with additional orientations as well as alternative typologies to describe the same beliefs—slicing the pie differently, in a sense. Below, we describe the two most common "add-ons" to the typology above.

Cognitivism

Cognitivists focus on information-processing skills and explain learning in terms of cognitive, or mental, ability and development. Based on the work of Piaget, Ausubel, Bruner, and Gagne, "interpretation, meaning, perception and insight are recurring themes in the cognitivist approach" (Magro, 2001, p. 77). Piaget's (1972) pioneering work that determined stages of development in the individual's ability to think was followed by Ausubel's (1978) position that teachers must help learners in developing their thinking skills by appropriately structuring learning activities to link new knowledge to old knowledge.

Constructivism

If there is a predominant philosophy hailed as foundational to online learning, arguably, it is constructivism (Mbati, 2013; Liang & Tsai, 2008; Yang, Yeh, & Wong, 2010). Following this perspective, knowledge is created among learners, working together, drawing on their individual perspectives and past experiential learning. Based on Vygotsky's (1978) work, constructivism also contains elements of Dewey's emphasis on the importance of learners' experience. This approach to learning serves adults well, both respecting their histories and fostering collaboration and creativity. However, as Rose (2013) points out in her excellent essay on reflection, today's emphasis on group interaction and collaborative knowledge-building lessens the time available for individual and quiet reflection by learners. She questions whether, in our move away from standardization and teacher-centred classrooms, "we have allowed the pendulum to swing too far in the opposite direction" (p. 75).

The philosophical orientations above are those used most often to explain, rationalize, criticize, or defend various approaches to teaching, learning, and assessment. But there are additional models and paradigms within which to understand learning. The pie can be sliced many ways.

We acknowledge Cross's (1981) delineation of barriers to learning: situational, dispositional, and institutional. We acknowledge Houle's (1960) typology that classified learners' motivation to learn as either goal-oriented or social activity–oriented, a combination of both, or simply learning-for-learning's-sake. We acknowledge Wlodkowski's (2008) classification of motivation into extrinsic and intrinsic and the grey areas in between. The complexity of the learning process needs all of these tools to facilitate understanding and, in turn, appropriately apply them.

We want to elaborate, however, on one more important classification of learning before discussing assessment in terms of one's philosophical beliefs. The concepts described in this system have already been outlined in previous descriptions above, but we feel it is important to present Habermas's typology in the following three terms as well: instrumental, communicative, and emancipatory. The discussion around these three types of learning is based on the fact that different kinds of knowledge necessitate different kinds of learning. The way we learn, and why we learn, as outlined above, affects the ways in which we should be assessed, if assessment is to be authentic and meaningful.

The German philosopher Jürgen Habermas held that individuals have three basic interests: "a technical interest in controlling and manipulating the environment, a practical interest in understanding each other and their social group and an emancipatory interest in becoming free from ignorance" (Cranton, 1998, p. 191). Pursuing each of these interests leads learners to a different style of learning. The "basic" learning is termed *instrumental*; this is the knowledge that permits us to exist in the world, to do things, to build homes, and so forth. To co-exist with each other in groups and in society, to make ourselves understood in order to accomplish our needs, we must communicate; hence, *communicative* knowledge. Communicative knowledge is clearly also practical, and its acquisition occupies much of our learning energy. Learners, regardless of discipline, must hone the ability to express their views and deal effectively with the interpretations and discussion that follow (Laurillard, 2012). But, beyond communication prowess—and reflecting Maslow's Hierarchy of Needs—human beings also want to achieve, grow, and self-actualize—they want to acquire knowledge and options to free themselves "from self-distortions and social distortions" (Cranton, 1998, p. 191). Critical reflection is the central process necessary in this type of emancipatory learning (Cranton, 1998; Magro, 2001; Plumb & Welton, 2001; Scott, 2006).

Critical Reflection: An Oxymoron?

We will establish here the importance of critical reflection in adult or "mature" learning, its role within constructivist environments, and its usefulness in online assessment. Rose writes about the importance of reflection: "Without reflection, it's almost like we're hollow" (2013, p. 35). This sentiment, somewhat akin to Socrates's words about the emptiness of "the unexamined life," questions the effects of not engaging in reflection. In her essay on reflection, Rose comments,

> I cannot imagine the work of esteemed critical thinkers such as
> Henry Giroux, Paulo Freire, and bell hooks, who strive to overturn
> existing assumptions about teaching and learning in our society,
> beginning in any way but with independent thought in conditions
> of silence and withdrawal. (p. 34)

Rose follows this by musing on the relationship of critical thought with reflection, pointing out that "critical" requires analysis and deconstruction, while reflection comprises contemplation and "inner" work. Nonetheless, she is clear that the apparent oxymoron does not diminish the credibility or value of the reflective process but rather accentuates how important it has become, and how entrenched it *should* become, to scholars and to learners. As humans, we are both rational and reflective; we can bring both those strengths to our teaching and learning. Rose makes a final, eloquent plea for the presence of reflection in our lives,

> It is only by opening ourselves to reflection, according it value as
> a way of thinking and being, that we can counteract the prevailing
> influence of the technical mindset, with its privileging of efficiency
> and instrumentalism, and thus achieve balance and fulfillment in
> our lives. (p. 35)

But what is reflection? Rose (2013) points out that this is a question well debated over the years, from pre-Renaissance philosophers through to modern poets. She arrives at a definition that emphasizes a type of sinking into deep and meaningful thought, with no impingement from the outside world: Reflection is a "form of deep, sustained thought for which the necessary conditions are solitude and slowness" (p. 3).

Similarly, Garrison and Archer (2000) suggest that reflection "is an integral part of all learning activities if they are to be educational" (p. 142). Schön (1983) further explores the nature of reflection, differentiating between two different kinds of activity: reflection-in-action and reflection-on-action. Reflection-in-action occurs mid-action when, all of a sudden, something unexpected happens and we must reorganize our "knowing-in-action"—our habitual responses—in order to make sense of the event (Garrison & Archer, 2000). Reflection-on-action is post-activity consideration of a completed event.

Can We "Cultivate" Reflection?

As teachers, we are often asked by learners if reflection can be "learned." Is it innate? Somewhat akin to the discussion on whether teachers are born or made, it is our opinion on this issue that reflection can certainly be fostered or, in Rose's (2013) terms, cultivated. Rose's take on the matter of cultivating the ability to reflect is intriguing, and perhaps romantic or idealistic (but who can blame an educator for dreaming?). She asks for the space and quiet to permit reflection, but she does not want to tag it as a problem-solving activity, because, she reasons, putting such restraints and guidelines around the process diminishes it. She does not want to see reflection used as a tool or a process, as "an approach to problem-solving nor a form of professional navel-gazing" (p. 102). Bereiter and Scardamalia (1987), on the other hand, define reflection as indeed a process: a "dialectical process by which higher-order knowledge is created through the effort to reconcile lower-order elements of knowledge" (p. 300).

The fact that scholars have identified two different approaches to the consideration of reflection does not in any way reduce its usefulness as a part of meaningful learning. And regardless of stance, Rose, Garrison, and Archer, in their respective works, share some techniques for helping to foster reflection in learners.

Education, Learning, and the Need for Reflection

Before elaborating on fostering reflective learning, we should sort out the terms *education* and *learning*. A common discussion in higher education classes revolves around the semantic differences among these two often synonymously used terms. We accept that education, broadly put, is a process of learning. Rose (2013) cites educational philosopher Maxine Green, who defines education as,

> openings, in unexplored possibilities, not in the predictable or quantifiable, not in what is thought of as social control. For us, education signifies an initiation into a new way of seeing, hearing, moving, feeling. It signifies the nurture of a special kind of reflect-iveness and expressiveness, a reaching out for meaning, a learning to learn. (p. 99)

But many would term what Green describes as simply learning. The visual below demonstrates a conceptual separation of education from learn-ing, where education is perceived as an external process that happens *to* the learner, and learning is perceived as an internal process in which the learner engages.

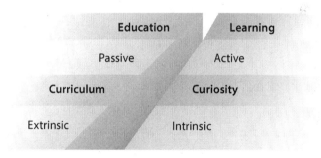

Figure 4.1. Education Versus Learning. Source: Holmen, M. (2014).

Within the realm of learning, on the journey to learning, reflection captures all the notions of terms like *intrinsic, curiosity,* and *active,* as listed above. Consequently, when the product of reflection is expressed in writing, Garrison and Archer (2000) picture that writing as "intentional, autonomous, rigorous and explicit" (p. 142). What, then, is the role of reflection in online learning?

The Role of Reflection in Online Learning

In Chapter 1, we discussed the pedagogy of online learning; in this chapter we have presented various philosophies of teaching and learning that should guide us in our practice. To those considerations, now, we add the importance of reflection. We are building the foundation for Chapter 5, in which we will discuss all these epistemological aspects of teaching and learning online as we outline our view of authentic, engaging, and quality assessment for online learners.

Although much of the seminal work on reflection is today perhaps attributed to Schön (1983), no one wrote more passionately about its value than the educational philosopher John Dewey. A pragmatist and a progressive, his views were complex and not without their critics (Garrison & Archer, 2000). However, he advocated ardently for many of the concepts that we hold dear today in higher and adult learning: collaboration, interaction, the sharing of control between teacher and learner, and a recognition of the value of the learner's experiential knowledge (Dewey, 1938).

Reiterating Dewey's beliefs about the importance of reflection, Garrison and Archer (2000) emphasize that reflection requires continuous judgment and insight. Even more telling to the importance of the reflective process, they continue, is that "the antecedent of judgment is the uncertainty of complex situations" (p. 22). Similarly, Brookfield (1990, p. 53) speaks of the power of "unexpectedness" in learning situations, where learners who have encountered an unintended challenge or obstacle remark in hindsight that such an occasion provided their best learning. Dewey, Garrison and Archer, and most constructivists call for knowledge-building situations that tax learners' comfort and their cognitive "place," and call on them to grow, use judgment, and reflect. The end-goal in advocating this stance is authenticity—of activity, and eventually, of assessment. In cementing his plea for interaction and reflection-generating learning, Dewey (1933) asked, perhaps rhetorically,

How shall we treat subject matter that is supplied by textbook and teacher so that it shall rank as material of reflective inquiry, not as ready-made intellectual pablum to be accepted and swallowed just as if it were something bought at a shop? (p. 257)

The affordances of online learning lend themselves so well to reflection. Consider first the technology. Online courses use Learning Management Systems (LMS) that are essentially text based. While multimedia—enabling audio podcasts, live chat and synchronous gatherings, video, YouTube, animated presentations, and all manner of graphics, pictures, and photos—has become a valued addition to earlier and less-sophisticated online offerings, the backbone of these platforms is still the written word. Writing words is a cognitive process that involves "intentional" and "deep" (Garrison & Archer, 2000, p. 141) actions—more so than orality, which often spills out without organization, complexity, or completeness. Time is the function at work here. Online learning, recognized to be, in many cases, more labour and time intensive than traditional face-to-face learning (Conrad, 2006), gives participants the time to consider what they are about to "say." There are a number of factors at work here, not all of them welcomed by learners: Typing words on a keyboard takes both time and skill; creating a posting online usually demands an edit before pressing the Send button; posting risks the chance of receiving questions or even negative feedback from others; and posting commits the words learners type to an archive for future reference and accountability, depending on institutional policy or the software itself. All in all, for many learners, especially the novice or insecure, writing online can be stressful and time consuming.

However, it also provides—*forces* upon—learners a vehicle to encourage them to think more deeply about the issues at hand than they may do in a face-to-face classroom, where a blurt or a nod can suffice for interaction and participation. While we don't assume that all online classes promote this type of deep learning, the potential is there, and an abundance of literature points out the online advantage (Garrison & Cleveland-Innes, 2005; Ravenscroft, 2011; Wang, Chen, & Anderson, 2014).

Another prime advantage of online learning is the exposure that each learner's thoughts can receive using LMS features, such as the discussion forum or conference, which are places where teacher and learners interact with each other and with the course material. The richness of this discourse depends on several factors, including course design, instructor approach to online teaching and "teaching presence," instructor expectations, and the resulting sense of online community (Conrad, 2005; Garrison & Cleveland-Innes, 2005). Online community, in turn, fosters a sense of safety and trust among learners as well as the fertile ground for higher levels of engagement in learning activities (Akyol, Garrison, & Ozden, 2009). Online "talking," therefore—verbalization via the written word—provides grounds for assessment. And whereas it's normal, perhaps customary, to award a portion of the evaluative grade for learners' participation in online courses, the largest portion of online evaluation in the social sciences and humanities will usually come from written work in the form of essays, tests, examinations, projects, or portfolios. Further discussion of strategies, rationales, and tools for assessment occur in the following chapters; assessment strategies for online discussion are discussed in Chapter 7.

Constructivism and Connectivism

Having discussed the role of reflection in online learning, we return now to a discussion of two philosophies that underpin and explain the online teaching-learning dynamic. For those whose task is to develop and design online courses, knowing the philosophy to which one adheres and the guiding framework for each pedagogical decision is key. But this book's topic is assessment, not course (or program) design, and we cannot enter into that very lengthy and complex discussion.[3] We do, however, discuss

---

3 Though we can suggest many related references, Terry Anderson's chapter, "Teaching in an Online Learning Context," in *The Theory and Practice of Online Learning*, 2nd ed., (2008) is useful, as is the entire third section in the same book, which is dedicated to the discussion of design of online courses. For novices, try Susan Ko and Steve Rossen's *Teaching Online: A Practical Guide*, 3rd ed. (2010) and Michael Moore and Greg Kearsley's *Distance Education: A Systems View of Online Learning*, 3rd ed. (2011) is a classic. The online ODL journal *International Review of Research in Open and Distributed Learning* publishes many articles on course

here the contribution of adult education and philosophical theory to the creation of online assessment instruments, specifically those that are intended to promote deep learning through collaboration and reflection.

Constructivism and connectivism are the guiding philosophies of choice for successful online learning and appropriate assessment strategies (Boitshwarelo, 2011; Ravenscroft, 2011; Siemens & Conole, 2011). We unabashedly endorse these approaches while acknowledging that there is still a role in online learning for other educational philosophies, such as behaviourism, cognitivism, and certainly humanism. Learning philosophies are not mutually exclusive, and the complex integration of factors that blend together to create any learning environment—a mix of the physical, emotional, social, cultural, and cognitive—permits a kaleidoscope of various potential situations in which learners engage. Garrison and Archer (2000) point out elements of cognitivism that can lead to an interpretation of learning as an information-process activity; similarly, elements of behaviourism lead to a doctrine of control and behaviour modification through environmental stimuli. From a broad educational perspective, both approaches "are reductionist in their views of learning" (p. 46). Humanism and its underpinning Rogerian psychology, in emphasizing personal growth and the potential for autonomy and self-direction, contributes to the constructivist tenet of respect for the individual's prior experience but does not speak to the collaborative and social aspects of knowledge building that must be central to online learning activities. Vygotsky (1978) was instrumental in marrying the concepts of cognition with social and cultural milieus. From this union came the notion of his Zone of Proximal Development and a theory of social cognition: "The zone of proximal development emphasizes the teaching-learning transaction and the socio-cultural context" (Garrison & Archer, p. 47).

Following on this is the constructivist tenet that "knowledge is a dialectic process [that] shifts attention from the mastery of content to the sociocultural setting and the activities of the people in a learning environment" (Campbell & Schwier, 2014, p. 359). More recently, Siemens

---

and program design, as does the *International Journal of E-Learning and Distance Education.*

(2005), collaboratively with Stephen Downes, has introduced the notion of connectivism, which he defines as,

> a process that occurs within nebulous environments of shifting core elements—not entirely under the control of the individual. Learning (defined as actionable knowledge) can reside outside of ourselves (within an organization or a database), is focused on connecting specialized information sets, and the connections that enable us to learn more are more important than our current state of knowing. (p. 7)

The principles of connectivism feature a distinct technological bent as well as containing bits and pieces of cognitivism, constructivism, and epistemological tenets. It has been suggested that, rather than a learning theory, it is more appropriately labelled a theory of how knowledge is distributed.[4] Nonetheless, the actions of knowledge being built, shared, and distributed are fundamental to successful online learning and therefore must be acknowledged, not only conceptually but also instrumentally, in design processes.

Aligning Philosophy with Design and Online Instruction

Campbell and Schwier (2014) note that critical theorists accuse instructional design of being prescriptive, restrictive, and reductionist, but they point out that a transformation that considers context, learning theory, an emphasis on sociocultural frameworks, and lifelong learning is underway. In other words, the effects of learner-centred learning theory, coupled with the increased effects of globalization and resulting cultural awareness and sensitivity, are shaping a changed sense of design. Assessment, as a part of design, will also benefit from this shift away from cognitive and behavioural learning design, where a focus on one answer, or the "right answer," gives way, where plausible, to responses that are socially or contextually constructed by learners.

Constructivist-inspired online activities and assessments will reflect various themes. At the most technical level, activities will make intelligent

---

4 There is some dispute over the status of connectivism and whether it is indeed a theory or a learning theory. See Downes (2011).

but accessible use of the technology available in LMSs. Those activities include encouraging collaboration and interaction within the course as well as constructing tasks that send learners out of the course—to other online resources, to simulations, to YouTube, to the many presentation tools that are available for educational use (Prezi, Emaze, PowToon, GoAnimate, and many more.)

At the instructional level, designers can incorporate opportunities for more autonomy for learners—choice of topic areas in which to engage, choice in selecting resources to access, and choice in participating in thematic discussions and conversation that permit the building of community among learners.

At the social level, designers can create spaces in which learners can virtually meet, engage, and share. Campbell and Schwier (2014) list the many informal spaces of virtual learning communities, beyond the sharing of knowledge:

- Spaces that allow learners to "know" each other and recognize their individual circumstances,

- Spaces that permit the building of social networks,

- Spaces that foster linkages among various cultural modes— language, politics, professions. (p. 366)

We acknowledge that assessment design is not the exclusive purview of course designers. Depending on the process in place at institutions of higher learning, individual instructors could well be responsible for developing their own courses and assessments. Subject Matter Experts (SMEs) could be hired for course development. The range of expertise and experience at work vis-à-vis pedagogical comfort could vary widely. We call for attention to not only instructional and design prowess but also to an insightful philosophical stance to guide both course development and presentation—and of course, assessment.

The Philosophy of Control

Dron (2007) highlights another lens through which to conceptualize assessment, terming it "control of the past" and describing it as "among the highest level of constraint in a traditional, institutional learning setting, guiding huge swathes of activities, acting as strong constraints and extrinsic motivators alike" (p. 101). Unfortunately, he is correct in many instances; his displeasure with the controlling aspects of assessment reinforces our own commitment to address the constraints of the traditional learning setting and challenge educators to break out of old restrictive patterns of assessment to recognize assessments as opportunities for learning and growth. Rather than using occasions of assessment as the "hammer," which Conrad's (2004) study of novice online instructors indicated was one perception of instructional power, assessment and its feedback should be couched in terms of support and potential enhancement of learning. Rather than rely on assessment to document the past, in Dron's language, use it as a building block to create a future of connection. Although there is no question that assessment feedback must point out errors and misconceptions, in what Garrison and Archer (2000) term "confirmatory" feedback (p. 162), it must also offer "explanatory" feedback in which misconceptions are analyzed and further "negotiation of meaning" is provided. Garrison and Archer point out that in occasions of higher-level learning, when tasks are less delineated and responses are expected to address more complex issues, explanatory feedback is essential for the learner.

The emphasis here, then, is less on control than on forward-looking growth in learners' ability to handle the material. While accepting the usually inevitable institutional demand for evaluation and the production of a grade, educators need not accept assessment as a constraint, but instead can employ it as a communication, a motivation, and a confirmation. Dron (2007) wryly admits that assessment has its uses and is a necessary part of the educational experience. Garrison and Archer (2000) see assessment as both challenging and uncertain. We agree that it is all those things.

The assessment process affects teachers as well as learners. As educators, we have experienced, often through reflection-in-action, epiphanies during the grading process, wherein our understanding of ourselves, our process, or of learners' learning becomes suddenly enlarged or perhaps clearer. Ramsden (1992) acknowledges and sums up the complexity of assessment and its many purposes, saying, "It concerns the quality of teaching as well as the quality of learning: it involves us in learning from our students' experiences, and it is about changing ourselves as well as our students" (p. 182).

Concluding Thoughts

This chapter opened with a discussion of the many and various philosophical approaches to teaching and learning. Constructivism was presented as a viable, and perhaps preferable, approach to teaching and learning online. To build knowledge in meaningful ways, it is necessary to help learners develop an appreciation of and ability to reflect on a process regarded more pragmatically by some (Garrison & Archer, 2000) than others (Rose, 2013). In overviewing the learning process, we distinguished between learning and education and then discussed the role and contributions of reflection in online learning. We outlined the need to align philosophy with both instruction and design, introduced Dron's (2007) criticism of assessment as a control mechanism, and countered with Ramsden's (1992) view of assessment as providing opportunities for knowledge building and growth for both learner and teacher.

4 | Authenticity and Engagement
The Question of Quality in Assessment

Authentic assessments, especially in blended and online learning contexts, encourage students to take a deep approach to learning, provide necessary alignment for faculty to better determine the quantity and quality of student learning, and provide institutions with the evidence necessary to respond to external pressures regarding their ability to measure student learning outcomes. This chapter defines authentic assessment, grounds it in constructivist theory, and considers some of the design considerations necessary to build authentic assessments that deliver on the promise of their potential.

Defining Authentic Assessment

Over 20 years ago, the "Principles of Good Practice for Assessing Student Learning" (Astin et al., 1992) were developed under the auspices of the American Association for Higher Education's Assessment Forum. These principles of good practice suggest that successful assessment begins with issues of use and then focuses on the issues relevant to educators and learners. Colby, Ehrlich, Beaumont, and Stephens (2003) suggest that assessment practices should assess students holistically, including "knowledge, abilities, values, attitudes and habits of mind that affect academic success and performance beyond the classroom" (p. 259). To assess these different areas, Astin et al., in their list of principles, recommended that assessment begin with educational values, and they caution that when values are skipped over, assessment diminishes to measuring what's easy, rather than offering a process that seeks to improve what's important to learners. Astin et al.'s principles further assert that assessment works best when it is ongoing, not episodic, when assessment reflects an understanding of learning as multidimensional, integrated, and revealed in performance over time; assessment also requires attention not only to outcomes but also and in equal measure to the performance that leads to those outcomes. These experiences should include "a diverse array of methods, including those that call for actual performance, using them over time to reveal change, growth, and increasing degrees of integration" (Astin et al, 1992). Authentic assessments fulfill the spirit of these principles.

Authentic assessments are based in real-world relevance. Authentic assessments include activities that closely match real-world tasks undertaken by practitioners (Herrington, Oliver, & Reeves, 2006). They are designed to actively engage students in their own learning by using real-life situations, requiring students to make connections and forge relationships between prior knowledge and skills, and allowing for multiple pathways for solutions and a diversity of perspectives (Moon, Brighton, Callahan, & Robinson, 2005). Authentic-assessment tasks are ill defined and "open ended, meaning that they can be solved through multiple approaches, mirroring what students will encounter later in life" (Moon et al., 2005). Authentic assessments are also highly engaging learning opportunities that can help foster students' higher-order thinking skills such as communicating, solving problems collaboratively, and thinking critically. Such skills support the new economy, which is characterized by "flatter management structures, decentralized decision making, information sharing, and the use of task teams" (Kay & Greenhill, 2011, p. 42), where such structures permit flexible work arrangements and encourage teams to work more creatively and productively, thus adding value to the workplace. Authentic assessments are frequently collaborative in nature, routinely using technology-rich co-construction environments (Barber, King, & Buchanan, 2015).

Other distinguishing features of authentic assessments include a longer and sustained time period and the use of multiple products, which can better gauge learner growth over time. According to Campbell and Schwier (2014),

> An instructor who assesses for authenticity either creates natural or real-life settings and activities or contextualizes learning in the settings that already exist in order to understand and document how learners think and behave over an extended period of time... the instructor uses multiple sources for gathering information that would reveal a more accurate picture of learning progress as well as emphasizing the process of learning, not just the final product. (p. 361)

Authentic assessments serve the interests of students by encouraging them to play a more active role in the assessment of their own learning through activities such as reflective exercises, self-evaluations in tandem with peer assessments, collaborative projects, semantic mapping, and e-portfolios.

A noteworthy characteristic of authentic assessment is its collaborative nature. Matuga (2006) writes that "situating assessment and evaluation as essentially social activities, influenced by unique affordances and constraints of a particular educational context, is a critical pedagogical component when designing and teaching online courses" (p. 317). This social, interactive dimension of meaning and knowledge construction is a suitable teaching approach for many areas, but especially for the growing focus on essential employability skills (Ontario Ministry of Advanced Education and Skills Development, 2015), which include communication (reading, writing, listening), gathering and managing information (selecting and using appropriate tools and technology, computer literacy, Internet skills), interpersonal skills (team work, conflict resolution), and personal skills (managing the use of time and taking responsibility for one's own actions, decisions, and consequences). Webb and Gibson confirm the value of collaborative, technology-enhanced learning, arguing that learning in technology-enabled collaborative environments requires cognitive, metacognitive, and social skills to develop "shared task understanding, negotiating shared perspectives, argumentation, and maintaining focus" (2015, p. 678). These complex cognitive skills are precisely the types of transferable lifelong skills highly desired in today's workplace by both students and employers.

Authentic assessment is especially important for many distance learners because, as adults, they are co-existing in twin worlds of work and learning (Campbell & Schwier, 2014). Such learners benefit most from assessments that as closely as possible replicate the task or process being assessed. And as authentic assessment is "connected to adults' life circumstances, frames of reference, and values" (Wlodkowski, 2008, p. 313), such assessments encourage participants to bring their authentic selves to the learning environment. Cranton and Carusetta (2004) define authenticity as a "multi-faceted concept that includes at least four parts: being genuine, showing consistency between values and actions, relating to others in such a way as to encourage their authenticity, and living a critical life" (p. 7). In authentic assessments, where students are called upon to work on real-life tasks with others, they are encouraged to bring their authentic selves, self-reflect on the congruence of their values and actions, and relate to others in authentic relationships. Because authentic assessments are open ended, based in reality, and frequently collaborative, they create the conditions conducive to transformative learning, where students, encountering alternative points of view and perspectives, come to question their assumptions, beliefs, and values, potentially leading to a change in world view and values (Kelly, 2009).

The Theoretical Foundations of Authentic Assessment

Authentic assessments emerge from constructivist and social-constructivist theory and from collaborative-constructivist transactional process models such as the Community of Inquiry. Constructivist pedagogies of active, interactive, and collaborative learning have proven effective in aiding student learning, so that, in recent years, positivist approaches to education and learning that objectified learning have ceded place to constructivist views. Constructivists emphasize the importance of creating meaning from personal experience and divergent thinking, and believe that many of the problems in current assessment practice can be overcome using a social-constructivist approach. Within the CoI framework, assessment is part of "teaching presence," the unifying force that "brings together the social and cognitive processes directed to personally meaningful and educationally worthwhile outcomes" (Vaughan, Garrison, & Cleveland-Innes, 2013, p. 12). Teaching presence consists of the design, facilitation, and direction of a community of inquiry, and design includes assessment, as well as course organization and delivery.

As noted in Colby et al. (2003), "the research literature on the effectiveness of pedagogies of engagement is extensive; it is also complicated because their impact depends on the quality and conditions of their use and the specific outcomes chosen to be assessed" (p. 136). While pedagogical effectiveness is dependent on a host of factors, Colby et al. posit that it is fair to say that when done well,

> teaching methods that actively involve students in the learning process and provide them with opportunities for interaction with their peers as well as with faculty enhance students' content learning, critical thinking, transfer of learning to new situations, and such aspects of moral and civic development as a sense of social responsibility, tolerance, and non-authoritarianism. (2003, p. 136)

McKeachie, Pintrich, Lin, and Smith (1987) include several studies highlighting key findings regarding the effectiveness of constructivist approaches. Gruber and Weitman (1962), for example, found that students who engaged in small discussion groups without a teacher not only did at least as well on a final examination as those students who sat in on the teacher's lecture but also surpassed their peers in curiosity (as measured by question-asking behaviour) and in their interest in educational psychology. Similarly, Webb and Grib (1967) reported on six studies that compared student-led discussions with instructor-led discussions or lectures and found that there were significant differences in achievement test results that favoured the student-led discussions. These two examples highlight the wealth of 50 years of research validating active and collaborative pedagogies. From the research, certain principles of learning have been developed:

1. Learning is an active, constructive process. In order to achieve real understanding, learners must actively struggle to work through and interpret ideas, look for patterns of meaning, and connect new ideas with what they already know.

2. Genuine and enduring learning occurs when students are interested in, even enthusiastic about, what they are learning, when they see it as important for their present and future goals.

3. Thinking and learning are not only active but also social processes. In most work and other non-academic settings, people are more likely to think and remember through interaction with other people than as a result of what they do alone.

4. Knowledge and skills are shaped in part by the particular contexts in which they are learned. Few skills are truly generic, and transfer of knowledge and skills to very different contexts is difficult.

5. One way to increase the likelihood that transfer will be successful is to make the context in which skills and knowledge are learned more similar to the settings in which they will be used. Another way to increase likelihood of transfer is by creating "the expectation of transfer" by making transferability an explicit teaching goal (Salomon & Perkins, 1989).

6. Reflective practice, accompanied by informative feedback, is essential to learning.

7. Chickering and Gamson's "Seven Principles for Good Practice in Undergraduate Education" (1991) encourages respect for diverse talents and ways of learning. Broadening the array of skills, tasks, and modes of representation used in a course increases the likelihood that students with different strengths will be able to connect productively with the work.

8. The development of genuine understanding is supported by the capacity to represent an idea or skill in more than one modality, and learning benefits from experiences that provide a wider array of modalities than those that usually dominate higher education (namely the linguistic and logical/mathematical). (Colby et al., 2003, pp. 136–138)

These principles highlight constructivist learning approaches, which form the foundation for the construction of effective authentic assessments.

Design Considerations for Authentic Assessment

There are several ways to create authenticity in learning and assessment. Reflecting the meaning of authentic assessment—assessment that values and connects to adults' life experiences and circumstances—educators can create assessment and evaluation tools that offer learners the opportunity to relate their learning to real-life subjects and real-life problems. Service learning, for example—where learners leave the classroom and engage in meaningful and authentic work in a community setting—offers a type of learning that is located in real time and is seen by some to provide a solution to perceived weaknesses in today's educational systems (Bok, 2006). Of service learning, Steinke and Fitch (2007) write that,

> because of [its] goal-based, real world nature, enhancing the quality of service-learning assessment can also provide a fresh perspective on the increasingly complex and often contentious assessment debates at colleges and universities across the country. The nature of service-learning often demands authentic assessments as faculty struggle to capture the real world transfer skills they believe are developing in their students. (p. 28)

Although the opportunities offered by service learning are not designed specifically for online learning, the philosophy and practice could easily be incorporated into online courses or programs. For example, with the same kind of preparation and structure as would be provided from classroom instruction, online learners could enter into a service-learning arrangement in their communities. The following are examples of potential service-learning experiences:

- Work on a Habitat for Humanity project constructing housing for families with low incomes

- Organize or assist with voter registration

- Work with a neighbourhood association

- Work with a public interest organization

- Work with a political campaign

- Assist with community events and projects such as museum activities, cultural awareness programs, fairs and festivals, Adopt-a-Highway, neighbourhood clean-up and beautification days

- Serve as a mentor for a young person through Big Brothers Big Sisters, Scouting, 4-H, or other youth organizations

- Help senior citizens with a variety of activities that enhance their quality of life

- Conduct a conservation project at a park, lakeshore, or nature centre

- Tutor elementary or secondary students in a variety of subjects, work with literacy, or serve as a "Reading Partner" to encourage youngsters to develop good reading habits. (University of Wisconsin–Eau Claire, n.d.)

Learners returning from their service-learning placements are assessed on their on-site experiences in relation to course learning outcomes that have been achieved. The blend of real-life experience with reflective activity, centred on expected outcomes, should produce a very authentic assessment or evaluation activity. In their report on service-learning assessment, Steinke and Fitch (2007) describe not only the virtues and appropriateness of authentic qualitative assessment but also present many qualitative tools that could be applied to measure service-learning outcomes.

To design an effective authentic assessment in any environment, one could ask, "How can I use assessment to encourage students to adopt a surface approach to learning, and then do the opposite?" (Wittmann-Price & Godshall, 2009, p. 216). Or, as Bull (2015) asks: "What is the absolute best evidence that learning has occurred for any particular learning outcome?" For carpentry students, the best evidence that they can plan and pour a suspended concrete slab is for them to plan and pour a suspended concrete slab. For paramedic students, the best evidence that they can respond to patients in crisis is to respond to patients in crisis, demonstrate the ability to remain calm in emergency situations, monitor patient vitals, and exercise judgment about what appropriate actions need to be taken, such as administering morphine alongside the presence of a preceptor so the patient is not put at unnecessary risk. Designing authentic assessments becomes more complex, however, when trying to assess higher-order cognitive skills such as critical thinking, problem solving, and communication. Critical thinking, especially, while frequently and intensely discussed among educators and researchers, remains a concept that eludes definition and assessment (Deller, Brumwell, & MacFarlane, 2015; Garrison & Archer, 2000).

Even though assessing higher-order cognitive processes and skills is difficult, it does not diminish the fact that design must commence with a focus on constructive alignment (Rust et al., 2005). Everything in the curriculum—the learning outcomes, learning and teaching methods, and assessment methods—should follow one from another and be connected in demonstrable ways. Learners should be able to see and understand the relationship between the parts of their courses. Learning outcomes serve as the roadmap to course content. They are broad yet direct statements that describe competencies that students should possess at the end of a course or program, competencies that show "what learners are supposed to know and what they are supposed to be able to do as a result of their learning" (Kenny, 2011, para. 1). Learning outcomes not only describe what students will be able to know or do but may also help students to understand how their course or their program will directly contribute to the competencies that are required of them in the workplace. Fuller discussions of learning outcomes and their contribution to authentic learning and assessment are found later in this chapter and in Chapter 7.

Addressing the need for the thoughtful design of authentic assessment, Gulikers, Bastiaens, and Kirschner (2004) developed the Five-Dimensional Framework for Authentic Assessment, a framework that includes essential planning elements to consider when designing authentic assessment: Task, Physical Context, Social Context, Assessment Result or Form, and Criteria and Standards. Building tasks for authenticity is essential for learners to engage with problems and tasks that replicate, as much as possible, real-life and professional situations. Herrington, Oliver, and Reeves (2006) suggest that authentic tasks support the learner by providing a meaningful context, enhancing motivation, supporting metacognitive development, and promoting transferability of learning.

The aspect of physical context has significant implications for all learners, but especially for distance learners, as there may be limitations in creating a truly authentic context, given the fact of the virtual environment. Physical context accounts for the relationship between where we are and how we do something. However, we could say the same for face-to-face learners as we question "whether assessing students in a clean and safe environment really assesses their ability to wisely use their competencies in real life situations" (Gulikers et al., 2004, p. 74).

According to Gulikers et al. (2004), assessment results include (a) a quality product or performance that students would be asked to produce in real life, (b) demonstration that permits making valid inferences about the underlying competencies, (c) multiple indicators of learning in order to come to fair conclusions, and (d) the expectation that students should defend their work to others to ensure that their apparent mastery is genuine. These expectations correspond to Herrington et al.'s (2006) perspective on the value of authentic tasks and their "polished products." Criteria and standards, therefore, become valued characteristics of assessments, with standards being the level of performance expected. Because employees usually know the criteria by which they will be judged, Gulikers et al. (2004) maintain that, for fairness and efficacy, it is important for teachers to set criteria and make them explicit and transparent to learners. Even more important than having criteria, however, is having students engage with criteria. A useful strategy for this is a marking exercise where students use a rubric to mark an exemplar. This exercise can deepen students' awareness of the standards by which they will be judged.

Tools for Authentic Assessment

There are several tools that can be useful for course designers in creating an environment in which authentic assessment gives learners a means of integrating assessment with learning, with real-life situations and with past experience. Feedback, as a tool, is considered separately below, as it occurs post-assessment. Both learning outcomes and rubrics should—ideally—precede assessment.

Learning Outcomes

Often equated to the behavioural objectives posed by Gagne (1971) and Mager (1997) decades ago, learning outcomes are a source of contention among educators. They are considered by some to be reductionist and narrow in their attempt to capture the breadth of learning in a succinct statement or two. Dron (2007) is highly critical: "Worse still, learning outcomes are fuzzy, context-related, and dubious constructs, at best and, at worst, absolutely meaningless" (p. 296). In the same criticism, Dron accuses learning outcomes of trying to bridge the gap between "knowing how" and "knowing that" (p. 296). We are particularly intrigued with this criticism, as it strikes at the heart of rigorous prior learning assessment processes that we endorse as authentic learning activities. Dron's contention, and the ability of prior learning processes to address this concern, are discussed in Chapter 5.

It may be true that poorly designed learning outcomes do not provide much assistance to the learning process in the same way that poor teachers do not add much to the teaching process and poor materials do not contribute to learners' learning. However, if we assume the presence of well-designed learning outcomes, outcomes that are not fuzzy or dubious, outcomes to which learning activities, materials, and ultimately assessments are aligned, then we accept that learning outcomes do indeed form an integral part of the learning cycle. Yogi Berra, that man of memorable words, famously said: "If you don't know where you're going, you'll end up someplace else." More poetically, and in the same vein, the author Reif Larsen (2009) speaks of maps in this way: "A map does not just chart, it unlocks and formulates meaning; it forms bridges between here and there, between disparate ideas that we did not know were previously connected" (p. 138). We consider learning outcomes as maps to learning. Garrison and Archer (2000) argue that properly constructed and applied learning outcomes align with a constructivist and collaborative learning environment. In keeping with this understanding, then, we note the encouraging integration of learning outcomes into quality assurance planning, program standards, degree qualifications frameworks, curriculum design, and transfer credit agreements (Deller et al., 2015).

The alignment of learning outcomes to activities, resources, and assessments is important to the integrity of the learning cycle. The role of learning outcomes in the alignment and planning process is discussed in Chapter 7.

Rubrics

Like learning outcomes, rubrics are contentious learning tools. As with learning outcomes, they are touted as useful guidelines for effective teaching and learning. And like learning outcomes, they are also considered potentially reductionist. As with anything, they can be rigorously and appropriately prepared, or they can be "fuzzy" and haphazard and therefore of little use. One of the better examples of rigorously developed rubrics are the 16 VALUE rubrics (Valid Assessment of Learning in Undergraduate Education) developed by the American Association of Colleges and Universities as part of the Liberal Education and America's Promise initiative from 2007 to 2009. Each rubric was developed to support essential learning outcomes, which reflect the most frequently identified characteristics of learning, having been tested by faculty at over 100 college campuses.

Ideally, a grading rubric tells students the goals, purpose, and manner of assessment: It states why the assessment is being conducted and how learners can succeed. The rubric should clarify curriculum objectives and provide criteria for meeting a range of proficiency levels (Mathur & Murray, 2006). We are of two minds about rubrics. As a tool and an aid to learning, they can indeed be helpful to learners in outlining the conditions of the assessment instrument and, as Mathur and Murray indicate, rubrics can guide learners in knowing how to complete the task successfully. However, all too often, rubrics are developed as a required add-on to assignments and follow a template that is generic, vague, and in its vagueness, open to the usual degree of subjectivity exercised by the marker of the assignment.

The examples that follow are actual rubrics, instructor-written and designer approved, for a university course. What does it mean to write, in a rubric: "Learners will demonstrate a high degree of comprehension of subject matter?" Similarly, consider this longer and more detailed rubric: "Content/ideas are thoughtful, relevant and presented clearly and logically. Assignment topics are coherently addressed and supported with relevant examples. Conclusion is relevant and insightful. Three or more references have been used appropriately." Even here, there is room for subjectivity in the assessment of relevance, thoughtfulness, logic, and coherence.

Subjectivity in the teaching-learning process is often regarded as the elephant in the room—more so in the social sciences and humanities than in the hard sciences, which is a discussion akin to the ever-present one around the "truthfulness" of both qualitative and quantitative research. There are also concerns regarding the "Gentleman's A" and grade inflation. We cannot deny our bias as teachers; the best we can do is understand it and address it by making it clear. Exploring and understanding our philosophical approach, as teachers, is key to this process. Medland (2010) concludes her study on subjectivity in assessment with the suggestion that understanding our own biases and subjectivity could help educators engaged in team marking find great "coherence." Educators who have participated in team marking will know, from experience, that the range of responses to learners' work by colleagues in the same discipline, content area, or field can be astonishingly varied. Bloxham (2009), speaking frankly, acknowledges that the topic of marking is under-researched and remains a "largely subjective process based on professional judgment grounded in assumptions of mutual understanding of disciplinary standards" (cited in Medland, 2010).

Wlodkowski (2008) explains what some instructors are doing when they do not use rubrics "formally" (p. 340). They are using them tacitly, or intuitively, making their judgments based on their professional experience and understanding of the topic, which would be captured in a rubric—if well written—but rather exists only in their heads.

However, another support for the use of rubrics comes from adult-education principles that emphasize autonomy and self-direction. Following this notion, the collaboration of learners with the instructor in the creation of rubrics supports constructivist thinking and fosters the building of community within the learning group. Another one of the benefits in having students employ the criteria and standards by which they will be judged in a marking exercise is the constant refinement of the rubric itself for greater clarity and appropriateness.

However, rubrics cannot overcome, diminish, or sidestep the marker's dependence on his or her own judgment, professionalism, and integrity. But in their defence, they can provide some degree of guidelines and rationalization for the forthcoming assessment to learners as they go about their work. On a cautionary note, however, Wlodkowski (2008) uses this analogy: "They're like a wall whose cracks you can't see until you get very close" (p. 341). By this he means that although the words on the page may seem concrete and make sense, the intricacy and complexity of assessment and performance is subtle, nuanced, and detailed, its actual demands eluding us until we are fully immersed in the "doing."

Feedback and Critique: Keeping the Learning Cycle Turning

Another important consideration in designing authentic assessments is planning for formative assessment and feedback. Given the variety of ways in which assessment can be used and the blurring of lines between summative and formative depending on that usage (see Chapter 1's discussion), "formative assessment" here refers to assessment that fosters a response to the learner, regardless of whether or not a grade is assigned to the work. Although some research argues that feedback is the most important factor in affecting future learning and student performance (Hattie, 1987; Black & Wiliam, 1998; Rust et al., 2005), other educators hold, perhaps more cynically, that the final grade is the telling factor for learners. Whatever the case, feedback—explanatory and confirmatory—is key to the cycle of authentic assessment. The most useful type of feedback is timely, detailed, and precise so that it can support learning. Such feedback helps clarify what good performance is; it facilitates self-assessment and reflection, encourages teacher and peer dialogue around learning, encourages positive motivational beliefs and self-esteem, provides opportunities to close the gap between current and desired performance, and can be used by instructors to help shape their teaching (Vaughan et al., 2013). Many students say they would like feedback more regularly (Colby et. al., 2003), and one of the great complaints by students of the reading of their assignments is that feedback is sparse or more confirmatory than explanatory.

Planning for the delivery of positive feedback to learners can help them succeed in their studies. Who among us has not received a paper back with only a checkmark on the last page and a grade? We are left to wonder what we did right and what we did wrong—or even if it was closely read at all. Positive feedback can help learners develop the self-confidence in themselves as competent learners; the resultant emotional dynamic feeds on itself, helping learners develop and maintain a learning pattern that fuels their efforts and carries them through the inevitable setbacks and hesitations that all learners face at some time. As assessment feedback contributes to the CoI's teaching presence, "instructors who take the time to acknowledge the contributions of students through words of encouragement, affirmation or validation can achieve high levels of teaching presence" (Wisneski, Ozogul, & Bichelmeyer, 2015, p. 18). The ability to both give and receive quality feedback is an essential communication skill in itself, as well as forming a component of authentic leadership (George, Sims, McLean & Mayer, 2011).

In addition to providing feedback, the constructivist approach that we have espoused requires that students actively engage with the feedback. Rust et al. (2005) cite Sadler (1989), who identified three conditions for effective feedback: (1) a knowledge of the standards in use; (2) comparison of those standards to one's own work; and (3) the required action to close the gap between the two. Vaughan, Cleveland-Innes, and Garrison (2013) suggest that, to promote student engagement by using feedback, "instructors in a blended community of inquiry are also encouraged to take a portfolio approach to assessment, [as] this involves students receiving a second chance or opportunity for summative assessment on their course assignments" (p. 93). Providing multiple opportunities to submit iterations of their work, and thereby encouraging students to work to close the gap between current and desired performance, is highly authentic and similar to real-world work contexts. Peer assessment (see Chapter 5) can also be a particularly useful approach to building a knowledge of standards, comparing those standards to a learning object, and providing students opportunities to engage with feedback and improve their work. As Nagel and Kotzé (2010) point out, "one of the strategies that can improve the quality of education, particularly in web-based classes, is electronic peer review. When students assess their colleagues' work, the process becomes reflexive: they learn by teaching and by assessing" (p. 46).

In summary, Reeves, Herrington, and Oliver (2002) have written extensively on authentic activities in online learning contexts, and the table below provides 10 characteristics of online tasks and the opportunities that authenticity should afford students, along with supporting research.

Table 4.1. Characteristics of Authentic Activity.

1	Have real-world relevance
2	Are ill-defined, requiring learners to define the tasks and sub-tasks needed to complete the activity
3	Comprise complex tasks to be investigated by learners over a sustained period of time
4	Provide the opportunity for learners to examine the task from different perspectives, using a variety of resources
5	Provide the opportunity to collaborate
6	Provide the opportunity to reflect and involve learners' beliefs and values
7	Can be integrated and applied across different subject areas and lead beyond domain-specific outcomes
8	Are seamlessly integrated with assessment
9	Create polished products valuable in their own right rather than as preparation for something else
10	Allow competing solutions and diversity of outcome

Source: Reeves, T. C., Herrington, J., & Oliver, R. (2002).

Concluding Thoughts

Recently, the notion of authentic assessment has become more central to higher education. The Higher Educational Quality Council of Ontario offered a three-part series on the challenges and opportunities in assessment in late 2015, and Educause offered a three-part digital badge series (entitled *Learning Beyond Letter Grades*), also in late 2015. Each series called for a move toward more authentic assessment strategies designed to increase learner engagement in the learning process at the same time as setting the stage for learners to develop higher-order cognitive skills that align with both learner and employer expectations. If assessment is the heart of the learning experience, assessment practices will need to encourage learners to bring their whole selves to engage with meaningful, relevant tasks to prepare them for a life of 21st century work and learning. Well-designed authentic assessments do just that.

5 | Assessment Using E-Portfolios, Journals, Projects, and Group Work

The shift to online learning in higher education creates a fertile environment for potential synergies between authenticity and assessment, and no better way exists to exercise authenticity in assessment than by portfolio. Here, we will refer to e-portfolios, which are portfolios that are no longer paper-based but are now mounted online, usually using a platform such as Mahara.

Simply put, a portfolio is a collection of parts, often called "artifacts," that has been constructed or compiled by learners wishing to demonstrate their competence in a certain area. While learning institutions use portfolios that are designed for knowledge demonstration, other types of portfolios also exist, for example, "showcase" or performance portfolios, designed to showcase individuals' value to their organization for purposes of advancement, to secure a position somewhere, or to peddle wares. Technology has accelerated portfolio popularity and purpose by creating many different platforms accessible for users who have no particular design skills.

Within educational institutions, portfolios have increased in popularity on many fronts. Many programs in universities have introduced portfolios as a means of assessing learners' aggregated work over the course term. Some graduate programs at Athabasca University, an open and distance university in Canada, have replaced comprehensive exams with portfolios.

Undergraduate programs have also implemented e-portfolios, reported by *University Affairs* (Bowness, 2014, para. 2) to be "way past trendy" now. Using the not-uncommon metaphor of a journey, students, through the portfolio process, are understanding their learning to be ongoing and sustainable. An undergraduate science student's e-portfolio at Canada's McMaster University is described here:

> His own e-portfolio exemplifies the tool at its best and most typical: blog-like, with banners, navigation menu and photos. Content-wise, Mr. Narro's e-portfolio includes pages detailing his employment and his academic and extracurricular activities, along with a section called "Courses" describing the nuances of his iSci program and another titled "Experiences" containing photographs and reflections on his geological field trips to places from Illinois to Iceland. (Bowness, 2014, para. 4)

The e-portfolio permits learners to accumulate, build on, and reflect on the shape of their learning experience throughout their programs, making cogent observations and connections among learning experiences over a period of time. Learners report benefit from their sustained engagement with the project and from having the time and the tools to reflect on their work and their progress. Officials from another Canadian university have indicated their interest in e-portfolios, as they are perceived to be "valuable beyond assessment. . . because you're able to see the whole person" (Bowness, 2014, para. 10). Additionally, in a very logistical but simplistic way, an e-portfolio mounted on the computer is more organic, colourful, modern, and exciting than a box full of collected papers to today's digital-native learners. What better way to authenticate one's learning and make sense out of theoretical or abstract knowledge in a day-to-day real world?

Recognition of Prior Learning E-Portfolios

Another very specialized use of learning portfolios in many educational institutions is for assessing and recognizing learners' prior and experiential or informal knowledge. Called by various names, the recognition of prior learning (RPL) uses a portfolio in which learners "collect, select, reflect, and project" (Barrett, 2000) the breadth and depth of their experiential learning according to standards and processes set by the institution. Naming conventions in the RPL world are important and often confused. An internationally applied process, RPL goes by a number of names. In Canada, it is referred to as both RPL and PLAR (Prior Learning Assessment and Recognition.) In the United States, it is largely referred to as PLA (Prior Learning Assessment). Elsewhere, in Europe, it may be called RPL or APEL (Assessment of Prior and Experiential Learning) or APL (Assessment/Accreditation of Prior Learning). Similar variations exist in Australia and South Africa. Depending on institutional standards, RPL processes can be arduous and taxing; accordingly, the credit reward allocation will also vary.

While the purview of this chapter does not include explicating the various systems or methodologies of RPL practice, which vary substantially around the world, we emphasize the value of this type of assessment given its authenticity; as well, RPL offers a good potential contribution to alternative methods of assessment in today's changing education world.

Good RPL practice holds that knowledge, once surfaced, must be presented in an acceptable format and then responsibly assessed so that learners receive appropriate credit for their prior learning. When learners' journeys are about and *of* their own experience, they are fulfilling one of the central tenets of authentic learning, which include the following:

- Authentic learning is "ill-defined," thus requiring learners to self-define tasks and activities.

- Tasks are complex and sustained.

- Tasks provide opportunities for applying multiple perspectives.

- Tasks provide opportunities for reflection and collaboration.

- Authentic learning surpasses specificity and can be both integrated into different areas and extended.

- Authentic learning permits a variety of outcomes and competing solutions (Reeves, Herrington, & Oliver, 2002).

The exercise of recounting and recasting one's prior learning during portfolio preparation reflects all aspects of authentic learning. Learners' prime focus is their own history. *They* are the subjects of their explorations. Their lives' events provide a tapestry of ill-defined activities that must be recalled, investigated, and understood for their learning value and placed conceptually and sequentially into various kinds of documents that usually include a narrative description and some form of explicit learning detail. Athabasca University has a very rigorous prior learning assessment system (http://priorlearning.athabascau.ca/index.php) that requires learners to produce a series of precise learning statements that are aligned with course and program learning outcomes and reflect various levels of learning achievement as set out by Bloom (1956) in his taxonomy of learning.

The timeline created by learners, from their past learning histories through to their vision of their learning future—which they are consciously working on and toward—creates a fabric of sustained engagement with their own learning and with "self." Self-reflection is key; meaning-making is one of the most difficult tasks in portfolio preparation. Meaning is internally generated from learners' own experiences. Those experiences must be "selected and collected" (Barrett, 2000), a process which, in itself, requires a degree of critical reflection and engagement with the larger, envisioned outcome.

As discussed in Chapter 4, Dron (2014) has accused learning outcomes of trying to bridge the gap between "knowing how" and "knowing that" (p. 296). Such confusion of purpose may be the case with many learning outcomes given the necessary specificity of language and the difficulty in obtaining such specificity and clarity from writers who may not be sufficiently trained in the nuances of language. However, careful application of Bloom's language from his taxonomy (1956) serves to differentiate types and levels of learners' knowledge, because some verbs point more directly to actions ("how") while others point to the possession of knowledge ("that"). For example, if I research a learning activity, have I designed it? If I designed it, did I create it? Or did I implement it *after* it was researched and created by others? In the RPL process, specificity of language carefully chosen by the learner is intended to demonstrate "knowing that," while the follow-up documentation of learning claims should affirm, by outside attestation, that the learner knew "how." However, we would agree with Dron when he says that examining the picky nuances of language is not an exact science in any of our work, and there exist many possibilities for looseness and error.

On the assessment side of this process, RPL practitioners often describe the process of externalization in metaphors of "yanking" or "pulling" learners' buried knowledge out of them as they prepare their learning portfolios for assessment (Conrad & Wardrop, 2010). This is difficult work for both learners and their coaches or mentors. The rewards, however, are sterling. Learners report high levels of satisfaction, revelation, and personal growth—in addition to the credit received as a result of their prior learning.

For their part, RPL assessors spend several hours with the e-portfolio.[5] A cognitively based task, their evaluation of the e-portfolio seeks to affirm a triangulated presentation of the learners' grasp of the importance and meaning of their prior and experiential learning. The articulation of their learning must, as an authentic product, situate the learning in a real-world time frame that shows growth and development; it must relate the learning to the external world, professionally and perhaps personally; it must project the potential for that learning into professional or life-related future contexts. Assessors must judge on issues of clarity, breadth and depth, relevance, and level of learning presented. That the demonstrated learning must be appropriate to the university study at hand is a basic tenet of prior learning assessment at institutions of higher learning.

Interestingly, assessors' comments indicate that they often feel affirmed and informed having read through a learning e-portfolio (Conrad & Wardrop, 2010; Travers et al., 2011). Learners' reflections and sense-making of their learning and career/life trajectories offer assessors new eyes through which to view their own practices or teaching. In this way, assessment continues to be about learning—for all those involved.

---

5 The authors are most familiar with an RPL process in which the terminology *assessor* is used. Similar processes sometimes use the term *evaluator*. As is often the case in these twin processes, both are in part correct. Further discussion on the importance of language in RPL processes can be found in Conrad (2011).

It is extremely difficult to falsify an RPL portfolio, and the fact of this provides further endorsement of the effectiveness of authentic assessment practices and of this type of document specifically. There are several reasons why this is the case:

- The e-portfolio demands a type of triangulation of data given its requirement for various artifacts to support each other: the learner's up-to-date resume; a narrative autobiography that outlines and highlights learning activities through learners' pasts; in the case of the Athabasca University model, extensive sets of learning statements detailing learning that can be documented in the resume; and items of documentation itself that are received by university personnel directly and can be verified and traced back to the originator of the document if necessary.

- The e-portfolio is a labour-intensive and time-consuming document. It is unlikely that an "imposter" could or would donate his or her time *over* a period of time to compile such a document.

- Learners become known to university staff in several ways. In some systems, there is face-to-face contact via office visits, webcam verification, or interviews. In other distance institutions, sustained contact via telephone—for mentoring purposes—establishes a relationship that is cemented with the exchange of many work and life details and the continual "yanking and pulling" of past learning from the learner that would render impersonation almost impossible.

- Learners, in conversation with prior learning personnel, are often required to discuss or reference their extant learning at the institution.

The engagement of learners with their learning is key to successful e-portfolio preparation and, hopefully, to a successful assessment by portfolio assessors. Learners, upon completion of their portfolio, usually report an experience that has been arduous and difficult, but also unique and personally rewarding (Conrad & Wardrop, 2010). The raising of self-esteem and personal confidence, and a new awareness of professional potential are also consistently reported by learners (Prior Learning Centre, n.d.).

Learning Journals

Just as the e-portfolio presents a sustained, dynamic, rigorous learning and assessment opportunity to learners, so too does the learning journal. Journals as learning tools are both loved and disdained by learners and teachers alike. Journal dislike arises primarily from several sources:

- Learners resent the amount of time that the journal *might* consume. (We write "might" because it need not consume an inordinate amount of time, although the potential is there, for those who are more naturally reflective than others, or for those who appreciate the scope that journals usually permit.)

- Some learners are uncomfortable being asked to write down their personal thoughts or opinions. A related source of concern with journals involves their assessment and learners' thought process that goes like this: *These are my thoughts; they are personal; they should not be reviewed for evaluation—or read by anybody, for that matter.*

- Some learners, in some programs, suffer from "journal fatigue," having been given journal assignments one too many times. And some learners have engaged in journal-writing processes that were not well disciplined or organized.

Like the portfolio, the learning journal asks learners to reflect on their learning over time, often over the entire duration of a course. Its purpose is to create a record of the learner's journey through the course and its materials and resources, including the insights that the journey has wrought; possible exchanges with other learners and with the instructor; and connections that the learner has made with his or her life, learning, and work. Most learning journals allow for a broad range of reflective material.

Journals offer the instructor or the assessor the opportunity to look for growth over time—growth in knowledge, in critical thinking, in the development of comprehension or appreciation of a topic. Journals can be structured so that learners are asked to follow a theme or a topic throughout the course, but the more effective journals, in our opinion, give learners free rein to create their own repository of reflections. Journals can also be used as a vehicle for instructor-learner conversation throughout a course—as a sustained activity whose purpose is the exchange, rather than an assignment that results in a grade. Or, perhaps both, reflecting again the complexity of formative and summative assessment.

Journals as Instruments for Assessment and Evaluation

We alluded above to the fact that some learners have concerns with the notion that the personal thoughts recorded in their journals are read by an instructor or that the journal is assigned a grade based on these musings or reflections. To the first concern, Fenwick and Parsons (2009) stipulate that the purpose of the journal should be made clear to learners. Instructors should clearly outline what they expect in the journal: That it is *not* a diary, that it is *not* a log of daily activities, and that is *not* a venue for personal confessional-type material. These are not difficult distinctions to establish, and good examples can be provided. Learners can be cautioned and guided to refrain from sharing sensitive material and still conform to the assignment's expectations, which may include a demonstration of attention to course materials, topics, and themes; critical thinking; and reflections by the learner on his or her own evolution or growth, in terms of learning, during the course.

There are other strategies that can be adopted to facilitate the assessing of journals. The suggestions that follow may address, to an extent, learners' concerns about privacy. One strategy involves requesting a short synopsis of the entire journal, perhaps two pages, about 500 or 600 words. Learners can be instructed to "highlight" their summary reflections in this short paper, to draw out the most important learning that they experienced, and to comment succinctly on the process of having engaged in sustained journal writing. Instructors can guide the structuring of this document by stipulating certain questions to keep the learner on track, for example: "How would you describe the most critical learning incident from this course?" Or, "What aspect of your course learning will you take forward as you continue your studies?" This document serves a couple of purposes. It forces the learner to revisit the lengthy journal and critically peruse it, and it forces the learner to be succinct and squeeze some very important concepts into few words. This is a process somewhat akin to guiding thesis- or dissertation-writing learners on the development of their research questions: It's hard to do, it's key to the success of the research, and well-written research questions usually require several tries.

The idea of creating a shorter document to capture the essence of the longer document involves grading. Instructors may wish to just assign a grade to the synopsized version, adhering to the rubric that has described its shape, thereby downplaying the sense that learners' feelings or personal musings are being evaluated. Again, how effective this result is depends on a number of factors that only instructor and learners can know. Or, instructors may assign an automatic "completion" grade to the actual document to acknowledge that requirements for the assignment have been met, while restricting judgment of the contents to a grade on the shorter paper. There are many variations of this theme. As always, however, the ultimate decision in both assessment and grading must reflect the course's intention and its stated learning outcomes; both assignment and assessment must complement the balance of the course's design.

Self-assessment is another strategy that can be considered in the management of the learning journal. Following a template provided by the instructor, learners use a close reading of their journals to respond to very specific questions that are designed to elicit some critical thought and analysis from the journal's contents. Learners assign themselves a grade for their journal; the instructor submits a grade for the summary response. As with all self-assessed documents, instructors should have in place a strategy for the self-assessment protocols. (See Chapter 9 for more on self-assessment).

Whatever the means of assessment adopted, instructors should take care to treat journals with confidentiality and respect the learner's work as a reflection of that person's experience in the course. Fenwick and Parsons (2009) suggest "liberating" learners from the academic-style correctness (APA, for example) that structures formal written assignments. Create a type of "free space" for creativity and personality.

Assessing learners' journal reflections offers instructors an opportunity to experience learners' insights of a nature and perhaps a scope that exceeds the confines of usual assignment topics. The well-done journal can turn a topic-related musing into an exploration of previously untouched thought. The sustained and consistent journal can document the progress of a learner's unfolding grasp of a topic, a learner's attempt at connecting disparate ideas toward theory-making, or a learner's struggle or success with conceptual material. And whereas wary learners may feel that journal assessments are sitting in judgment of their feelings or opinions, rigorous and appropriate assessment should be an evaluation of thinking, application, analysis, and synthesis—in fact, an indication of Bloom's (1956) cognitive levels. The rubric that accompanies journal assessment should indicate the structure and outcomes that the assignment calls for.

Journal Rewards

The rewards, for both instructors and learners, of journal writing have been hinted at in the sections above. This assignment provides latitude for learners to exercise creativity, introspection, and thoughtfulness—infused with personality—while attending to course themes but not being restricted by narrow parameters. It allows them to draw the course content into their own thinking and experiences, and vice versa. It can manifest in Vygotsky's Zone of Proximal Development or produce the fruits of shared knowledge building, revelation, even transformation, which, as Mezirow (1997) understood it, is a changed perspective slowly developed in learners over the duration of a course.

For instructors, the journal often opens the window into the mechanics of a learner's learning. Like the curtain being lifted on the Wizard of Oz, instructors can glimpse the inner workings of the learner's process as he or she has lived it. This offers a type of insight that is rarely afforded the instructor when learners are asked to write on an assigned topic. Logistically, however, if a journal is submitted at the end of the course, the insights and revelations that so often are unveiled come too late for instructors to act upon or acknowledge, except in feedback on that particular document. Conversely, to take the journal in after a shorter amount of time could deprive learners of the chance to develop and expand their thinking to an optimal degree.

Projects and Group Work

When is group work *not* group work? When it's a project! While this version of the old joke is not quite true, it can be made to be somewhat true in that the abundance of media tools available to online learners permits a wide range of exciting activities that learners find enjoyable and worthwhile. Many students simply say that learning is fun when they can step away from problem sets or research papers and actually engage with materials or tools. As Windham (2007) points out, they relish the opportunity to be creative, to build, and to experiment with Web-based presentation tools, mind-mapping software, YouTube, video clips, audio enhancements, and graphics. While this is not intended to be a comprehensive list, it points to the vast choice available to learners to enliven a project assignment. Such media-based assignments can be done solo, but the dynamics of group work offer learners much more opportunity for creativity, collaboration, and knowledge building. The solo project is often just an assignment with another name—a piece of work constructed by one learner to complete a task whose purpose it is to demonstrate mastery or comfort with course material. It is the group work project that usually attracts the most attention—and the most disdain.

Group Work Challenges
Roberts and McInnerney (2007) tackle the issue of group work in "Seven Problems of Online Group Learning (and Their Solutions)," naming the problems as follows (p. 257):

- Student antipathy to groups
- Selection of groups
- Lack of group skills
- The "free rider"
- Inequalities of student abilities
- Withdrawal of group members
- Assessment of individuals within the group.

As they point out, these problems are interrelated and often causal. Roberts and McInnerney (2007) identify the assessment of individuals within groups as the primary group work issue. Based on our personal experience, that may well be true, but the interrelatedness and causality of group issues make the problem of assessment even more nuanced and difficult. Over what factors does the instructor have control in her groups? Where does her skill and experience most come into play? How can she become aware of a problem before a group's dynamic deteriorates and learners are put into a potentially harmful social situation? When should she intercede?

In our experience, learner antipathy to group work is historical, usually the result of previous bad group experiences. Bad experiences, in turn, often result from inequity in group members' skills, the "free rider" phenomenon, and perhaps the unanticipated withdrawal of group members. While instructors can blithely guarantee their learners a better experience "this" time, care must be taken to put measures in place that will foster constructive group activity. Some group work issues are discussed in the following section.

Selection of Groups

Group member selection is one of the ways to improve the group process. While acknowledging that random selection can sometime work just as well as anything else, Roberts and McInnerney (2007) argue that deliberately selecting a heterogeneous group is the best solution. In this way, the levels and diversity of experience are mixed, and the possibility of ending up with cluster of similar backgrounds, geographical locations, or some other circumstance is avoided. Another useful strategy is to allow learners to self-select their groups further on in the course, when they are more cognizant of their peers' learning styles. Watchful instructors, however, must be wary of clique-ism and the possibility of exclusion of members from groups.

Differences or Lack Thereof in Group Skills

This problem can, in part, be considered in terms of "inequality of student abilities." We must assume, as a starting point that each class is going to contain a variety of abilities, strengths, and weaknesses. A deliberate selection will in most cases result in a mixture of abilities within the group. Some learners will learn from other learners. Some learners will be frustrated with the input of other learners. From our own experiences both as teachers and learners, we see this as inevitable. To counter these effects of inequality as much as possible, the instructor will explain the function and expectations of the group as clearly as possible and perhaps outline some ground rules for process. That process may include reporting on group progress. It may include assigning learners to specific roles within the group or asking that roles be selected internally by the group without assistance from the instructor. Learners can also be directed to literature on group function, in some easy-to-access "how-to" format.

Regardless of instructional efforts, groups will most likely produce a leader and some followers, some happiness and some unhappiness. It is often the case that those who are initially unhappy will admit to a satisfying outcome once the process has concluded and, with sound direction and some good fortune, the group has succeeded in the task. Response to and reflection on the group process can often be found in learners' journals, when journals are used as ongoing documents constructed throughout the course, as described above.

The "Free-Rider"

Every learner and instructor is familiar with this issue. Perhaps you have experienced it yourself; as an instructor, you have no doubt had learners complain to you about their "free-riding" group members. Tied in to group members' abilities, life's vagaries, and general inequality, the group member who does not pull his or her weight is all too common. Roberts and McInnerney (2007) suggest two alternative forms of pressure that can be applied to address this issue. Pressure can be applied to group members in the form of instructional pressure—through specific assignment of roles or detailed instructions—or peer pressure, which equates to giving permission to group members to either voice their dissatisfaction, privately or publicly, or self-assess the group's functioning. Group members self-assessing on group performance need not be synonymous with evaluation. Qualitative input can suffice. All these strategies can be uncomfortable for learners (and for instructors) and require tact, respect, and careful instruction.

Assessment of Individual Group Members

Does it ultimately come down to this? Many would say, "Yes, individual assessment of *my* effort in the group is what works best, is what is fair." Supporting this reasoning, Roberts and McInnerney (2007) cite literature that maintains that "assigning group grades without attempting to distinguish between individual members of the group is both unfair and deleterious to the learning process. . . and may in some circumstances even be illegal (!)" (p. 264). Webb, however, counters that the "purpose of assessment is to measure group productivity" (Webb, as cited in Roberts & McInnerney, 2007, p. 264), highlighting the need for measuring learners' ability to interact, coordinate, cooperate, solve problems, and resolve conflicts. Does peer-assessment or self-assessment adequately address those outcomes? They could. How can these "fait accompli" processes, already accomplished by the time the instructor receives the finished product, be properly measured?

This nest of situations creates one of the differences in procedure between face-to-face learning, assumed to take place in a bounded environment—a classroom—and online learning and its unbounded space. In the former learning environment, it may be possible for a teacher to observe a group's interplay and activities or to, in some way, ascertain how the group is functioning (or not) together. (Whether the instructor chooses to act on these insights or observations is another matter.) However, no such prerogative exists online. Without the ability to receive insights or data from observation or physical presence, if a judgment on group process or individual contribution to process is required or desired, instructors must implement measures to receive such data. Some options include,

- *Assessment of an individual's contribution to a group project.* To conduct such assessment, learners submit a report on their own contribution to the group project, along with—most likely— evidence of that contribution.

- *Peer assessment of individuals' contributions.* In this case, each member of the group submits an assessment of each member's contribution. To many instructors (and learners), this may seem indelicate. To ameliorate potential feelings of "unpleasantness," instructors might supply a template or form that contains a rating scale and space for comments.

- *Self-assessment.* Each learner would submit to the instructor a self-commentary on his or her contribution. A variation of this option is to have learners make these decisions among themselves prior to submission.

- *Progress reports.* Each term, depending on the complexity and scope of the task, learners provide weekly progress reports of "chunks" of the assignment for review and revision. This process may enable the instructor to become aware of potential problems sooner rather than later. Progress reports also highlight the importance of the process rather than the product.

In each of these situations, instructors can blend, in some reasonable proportion, the collective grade for the completed project with these data from individual assessments. There is no "easy" way to collect this data. Somewhere, somehow, some hard decisions and reporting must occur. Making all the conditions of assessment clear to learners before the activity commences is critically important for fairness. Such clarity should enhance performance and lead to superior outcomes and less "free-ridership."

Roberts and McInnerney (2007) suggest a method whereby each learner submits a pie chart diagram indicating percentages of members' contributions. They propose that this activity be done individually, and they comment that this system works well.

Group Development

Tuckman's (1965) seminal research outlined the stages of group formation and performance. Garrison and Archer (2000) refined group understanding in a more precise, education-related fashion, using Pratt's (1981) work. For these educators, groups have three stages, the first of which compares to Tuckman's "forming" stage, where clarity of instruction and purpose is of prime importance. Learners need to know, and focus on, the intent of the group and the task at hand. Once past this stage, learners tackle the work ("performing") and must address all the challenges that come with producing a product as a group. They will, understandably, experience conflict, negotiation, reconciliation, and cohesion.

The third and final stage of group development is termed "ending." Assessment—and the apprehension of assessment—forms a part of the ending stage. Closure and acceptance also form part of the "ending"; a well-defined assessment plan will help with both those aspects of winding down the group project.

Problems and anxiety aside, group work can provide constructive and positive outcomes to fulfill the constructivist mandate. Given a content-related but ill-defined topic, and the encouragement to use concrete examples, learners working together as a group will bring their own experiences to the assignment. The group project, enacted in this way, provides many benefits to both learners and instructor:

- Learners extend out of the usual text-based realm, creating new interest in the task.

- Learners can demonstrate a new range of skills brought to the fore by working in a new media environment or with new tools, whatever they are.

- Peer appreciation of others changes or grows.

- Tech-savvy learners teach other learners new software or tools; each learner feels empowered.

- The opportunity or need to research course topics beyond assigned readings or textbooks introduces some learners to topic knowledge that might have gone unnoticed.

- Learners practice group learning skills, organizational skills, and personal skills.

- The presentation of the final project online affords learners another opportunity to explain and promote their work; it affords the group "audience" another opportunity to observe and reflect on the thinking and the process of others; and it affords another lens into the application of an authentic response to the topic.

Garrison and Archer (2000) stress the need for authenticity within the group, especially for the group leader, so that the prevailing attention-to-task and resultant engagement can facilitate the group's work. A "group leader" can refer to the instructor, who is ultimately responsible for assigning groups, roles, and tasks, or to a student leader within the group. In the case of the latter, some specific instruction from the instructor in leadership or group expectations would serve well if the role is to be well executed. Singer, Astrachan, Gould, and Klein (1975, as cited in Garrison and Archer, 2000) suggest that a good group leader is task oriented and focuses on the agreed task at hand.

Concluding Thoughts

E-portfolios, journals, projects, and group work all provide opportunities for learners to authentically engage with learning materials and, likewise, to be assessed for meaningful and authentic performance. E-portfolios are becoming increasingly useful in many different environments, RPL being one of them. E-portfolios are also serving graduate learners as authentic vehicles for the demonstration of knowledge, often replacing comprehensive exams. Projects and group work have long formed parts of assessment strategies and are no less useful in online learning than in face-to-face courses. On the contrary, access to innovative media increases the attractiveness of project use in online learning, although the fact of "distance" decreases instructors' ability to observe group process, therefore *increasing* the need for adherence to well-explained and well-understood assessment processes.

6 | The Age of "Open"
Alternative Assessments, Flexible Learning, Badges, and Accreditation

The ancient curse "may you live in interesting times" could adequately describe the dilemma that has confronted institutions of higher learning in the past decade or so. Not only have the stalwart halls of traditional learning faced, and adapted to, online learning and virtual learning environments since the late 1980s, they have also, more recently, been bombarded with the antithesis of higher education: courses purporting to enrol thousands of students who will pay no tuition and never step inside a classroom. MOOCs (Massive Open Online Courses), pushing at the walls of higher education in unprecedented fashion, have been offered by institutions of the highest calibre (Stanford, MIT, the University of Toronto, Harvard, and many others) and sparked new levels of discussion that centre on the roles of education and educators, while also uncovering the philosophies underlying higher education, including those that guide assessment and evaluation.

As a part of the ongoing MOOC discussion, Davidson (2014) outlined her view of their limitations: They are not going to remedy higher education's problems, which she describes—referring to the United States—as a "product of 50 years of neoliberalism, both the actual defunding of public higher education by state legislatures and the magical thinking that corporate administrators can run universities more cost-effectively than faculty members."

Davidson appears to be correct. The largest study so far into who enrolls in MOOCs, and why, suggests that participants are mostly well educated and employed individuals in developed countries and that "the individuals whom the MOOC revolution is supposed to help the most—those without access to higher education in developing countries—are underrepresented among early adopters" (Christensen et al., 2013, p. 1). The magical thinking that MOOCs, or any technological solution, can solve existing power differentials does not address the fact that educational opportunity, often based on standardized assessments, maintains and reinforces an unequal playing field.

> In a society where people start out unequal, educational opportunity—especially postsecondary educational opportunity dictated by test scores and grades—can become a dodge, a way of laundering the found money that comes with being born into the right bank account or the right race. As social science has proven, the meritocratic basis of education is, at least in part, a social construct. Education is itself stratified by race and class, ultimately creating a hierarchy of educational inclusion that confers public and private power over others. A vote is not worth nearly as much personal power over others as is a college degree leading to a well-paid professional occupation. *Testing and all the other metrics that allocate educational opportunity are better social indicators of our collective failure to provide equal opportunity than measures of innate individual merit or deservedness.* (Carnevale, 2016, p. 22, emphasis added)

MOOCs, with improvements in instructional design and a gain in recognition, may eventually take an important place in the educational landscape. In an odd twist, MOOC participants tend to themselves be educators who satisfy their curiosity and gain new ideas for instruction (Newton, 2015) from their MOOC participation, which may in part explain the high attrition rate from MOOCs, where participants leave the course once they have obtained what they "need." But the long-term possibility that MOOCs will deliver meaningful educational opportunities to the least privileged, such as English language learners or the digitally unprepared, seems remote. This is also the studied opinion outlined in Sir John Daniel's

2012 South Korean report, in which he concluded that "the discourse about MOOCs is overloaded with hype and myth while the reality is shot through with paradoxes and contradictions."

All this being said, however, two things have become very clear during the turmoil that MOOCs have wrought: Firstly, the pedagogical nature of distance and online learning has not been well understood within higher education; and secondly, the role of assessment within learning remains paramount and complicated. Issues of assessment, in fact, have been the source of much of the furor around the potential acceptance of MOOCs into university programs. This chapter will consider the role of assessment in open and alternative learning. We have already considered the role of traditional assessment and its role in the learning cycle. Has that changed? *Should* it change? Will the champions of the Open Education Resources (OER) movement drive their mantra of openness right through established assessment protocols? UNESCO has now appointed three OER Chairs, worldwide. How will this political—and seemingly trending—endorsement of openness affect higher education's approach to assessment?

Disruption and Assessment in the Age of "Open"

MOOCs represent only one aspect of the shifts to "open" that are ongoing in today's higher education. There are more shifts, all signalling changes that affect the business of institutional learning on a macro level that exceeds our focus here on assessment. In the discussion that follows, we consider several elements relating to assessment as it is disrupted or challenged in light of the shift toward "open."

The broader trend underpinning these shifts in educational culture can be labelled "popularism." In a recent essay, Shea (2014) refers to the currently popular TED (Technology, Entertainment, and Design) talks, noting that today's academic "celebrity" is viewed on TED stages in 18-minute bites, "upending traditional hierarchies of academic visibility and helping to change which ideas gain purchase in the public discourse." One of the results of this popularization is the "flattening" or down-sizing of ideas; the result is a "quick-hit, name-branded, business-friendly kind of self-helpish insight" (Shea, 2014). Consequently, he argues, the decline of theory in favour of a new "life-hacking culture" has enhanced society's potential for productivity, achievement, and quick gain. Similarly, Rose describes our current society as running at "twitch-speed" (2013, p. 8). Although it should be noted that this trend is not disparaged by all and is in fact welcomed by some who are weary of philosophical long-windedness. The salient point here is that notions of assessment within higher education are assimilated and affected by the spill over of these broader trends. An examination of how resultant innovations bear on evaluation and assessment strategies in higher education follows.

MOOCs and OER

These closely related phenomena have presented twin challenges to higher education's traditional operations. As discussed above, the sudden emergence of MOOCs and the immense controversy (and confusion) generated by them have initiated intense scrutiny, not just of "how" to deliver courses but also of the place and meaning of higher education in our lives. What is the current state of MOOCs? At the time of writing, their juggernaut has lost some of its thrust, but in its wake, there remains both some activity and new research into the nature of the phenomenon (Kolowich, 2014). In a study cited by Kolowich (2014), results showed, among other things, that students learned as well in MOOC courses as in traditional courses, and that the professoriate could either save time, by using already-developed or accessible resources (an OER or an entire MOOC) or expend *more* time, by having to adapt materials to already-existing courses. What was not raised in the research was the issue of assessment and credentialization—the difficulty inherent in assessing performance in MOOCs and the larger difficulty of accrediting MOOC learning to a formal credential. Assessment, and subsequent recognition of performance, has already been identified in higher education as the highest hurdle to cross (Conrad, 2013; Friesen & Wihak, 2013).

OER offer a more understandable and narrower focus for educational change. OER refers to the creation of educational resources (modules, lessons, curricula, video, podcasts, graphics, animation, and, potentially, assessment design) that are made widely available by OER creators. The intent of OER advocates is to facilitate the introduction of multifaceted resources into course production in financially feasible ways. Weller (2011) acknowledges that freely available academic content not only removes many types of restrictions and limitations on the accessibility of resources but also supports constructivist thought in that knowledge is truly constructed rather than simply accessed, passed on, or delivered.

Flattened Hierarchies, Crowd-Sourcing, and Crowd-Teaching

Together, these relatively recent "facts" of educational life are subsets of the wave of openness that attempts to flatten the traditional hierarchical structures of the Ivory Tower. In one way or other, each asks the question: Why should one person be privileged or stand above others? In academia, the "standing above" usually amounts or equates to assessment. Why should *you,* for example, as a journal editor, tell *me* that my work is acceptable or not acceptable? Why should *you,* as teacher, tell *me* what I should learn from this source or about this topic? Clearly, evaluation and assessment as it has been known and observed in higher education is facing pressure in light of the open movement.

Peer Assessment and Peer Evaluation

Peer assessment may be the oldest and most commonly used of these new developments in assessment techniques. No doubt most educators have used some sort of peer assessment in their classes at some time. Examples are numerous: Let's have a debate and the class will vote on which side wins; let's do a role-play and let the class decide who has been most effective at portraying a historical figure; after our projects have each been presented, each class member will complete an "evaluation" form outlining the strengths and weaknesses, high and lows, of each presentation.

The jury is out on peer evaluation and assessment in the literature, although good practice recognizes that there is pedagogical value in engaging learners in self- and peer-assessment at a formative level. Race (2001) outlined several aspects of the positive contributions of peer assessment to learning:

- Students are doing it already in different ways.
- Students will get the chance to find out more about assessment culture.
- Lecturers have less time to assess than before.
- Learning is enhanced when students have contributed to their marking criteria.
- Assessing is a good way to achieve deep learning.
- Students can learn from the successes of others.
- Students can learn from other's mistakes. (pp. 94–95)

Until the emergence of MOOCs, summative peer assessment or evaluation was rare in traditional classrooms. However, following on the heels of the reliance of MOOCs on learners to initiate and lead activities among its thousands of enrolees, peer assessment became a MOOC staple, for example, in Coursera courses (Cronenweth, 2012). Sometimes software-assisted, sometimes permitting written commentary, the use of peer assessment, in our opinion, has limited value and limited reliability when used *summatively* (and hence becoming *evaluation*). Value and reliability are further limited in courses designed for seeking, or intended to seek, credit toward a postsecondary credential. In stating this, we do not disparage teaching and learning philosophies that value group work and learner collaboration, or constructivist principles that value learners' prior experience and encourage learners to bring that knowledge forward in the creation of new, shared knowledge within the group; it is often noted that "peer assessment is an important part of a shift towards more participatory forms of learning in our schools and universities" (Kollar & Fischer, 2010). However, encouraging student engagement and participation—and thereby, one hopes, cognitive growth—within an instructor-designed or instructor-led framework is a far cry from instructor abnegation. Brookfield (1990b) famously stated that teachers or instructors had a moral obligation to give something of value to their learners. Whether labelled teaching, instructing, or even facilitating learning, Brookfield cautioned against the role of teacher devolving to that of gatekeeper.

On the topic of instructor engagement, and referring to peer assessment, Cronenweth (2012) asked: "This form of 'crowd-sourced commentary' helps create a learning community—so why not build the community even further by empowering learners to evaluate one another?" The abbreviated answer, from our point of view, is simply that learners are learners because they do not yet have the scope or depth of relevant knowledge that teachers do. In many cases, as well, they lack the skills to manage the classroom and its processes—whether face-to-face or online—effectively. To this end, instructors of non-MOOC online classes—the kind we were used to before the MOOC juggernaut—know that they must be regularly present in order to prevent "crowd-sourced commentary" from going off the rails or from careening down a tangential or erroneous path that has been instigated by a poorly informed member of the group, however well intentioned. As for MOOCs, the fly in their ointment has been, from their genesis, finding a way to conduct rigorous and reliable assessments and evaluations that are acceptable to other receiving institutions in the interests of receiving credit for completed MOOC courses.

Open Access Journals

Open access journals, while no longer the new kid on the block, owe their existence and rising popularity to the open movement. Currently, most such journals make their content freely accessible through electronic sites but still engage in the traditional processes of blind peer review of submitted manuscripts. Research shows that the peer review aspect of open access journals is still highly valued by the academic community (Edgar & Willinsky, 2010). Assessment in the traditional sense is still at play here, although the breadth of the process, of necessity, makes it more democratic and less hierarchical than, for example, a typical teaching situation where one instructor/professor/teacher is responsible for allocating grades to many learners. But the call is heard for changes to journal processes. A number of open access journals, including *arXiv* and *PLOS,* have experimented with alternatives to traditional peer review, in an effort to determine whether an open peer-review process can sustain the appropriate level of academic integrity and rigour. These experiments seek to answer a question posed by Chris Anderson (2006): "Who are the peers in peer review?" Evaluating the pros and cons of an open review process, Tom DeCoursey (2006) writes,

Reviewers can give their expert opinion, which might be honest, tainted by emotion, or even an overt attempt to suppress the manuscript. The authors can rebut these arguments. But it is the editors who must determine whether the reviewer has noble motives.

And then what? After a period of robust "he said/she said" volleying of opinion, an *evaluation* must be made upon the worth of the work for publication. Someone must do this! DeCoursey (2006) ultimately admits that the summative process of an open-style review can provide value to the article (optimally, that is the function of the current peer-review process) but concedes that perhaps there is a place for anonymity in the case of rejected articles. DeCoursey concludes that this might be for the best, reinforcing the notion that assessment as evaluation is a difficult task, even a moral responsibility—a sometimes unpleasant task that must reside *with* someone.

Social Media and Crowd-Sourcing

Years ago, while teaching English at the college level and using Orwell's *1984* as an example, we used to awaken the critical consciousness of young learners to the dangers of "crowd-speak," that is, to the danger of being coerced or unduly influenced by what others were doing or saying. In an ironic reversal of social mores, technology and social media have created an environment where both seeking and making possible the opinions and input of others is not only acceptable but often demanded. There is some justification for this trend, as shown in many instances where Twitter, for example, has been an effective medium for disseminating useful information and for helping individuals engage in and contribute to useful social and community endeavours.

However, for purposes of academic learning, does social media's "even playing fields" contribute to a quality, or even acceptable, learning experience? The answer to this is a work in progress. Wikipedia is a good example. Current opinion has it that Wikipedia, once scorned by academics, has become, and is becoming, more acceptable. While the watchword on its use remains, sensibly, "use critical judgment," the take-up of Wikipedia by reputable academics has increased in recent years. And while the fact of its lack of peer review is still an issue cited as a factor against its credibility, the argument once again comes down to one's view of openness,

> The openness of Wikipedia is instructive in another way: by clicking on tabs that appear on every page, a user can easily review the history of any article as well as contributors' ongoing discussion of and sometimes fierce debates around its content, which offer useful insights into the practices and standards of the community that is responsible for creating that entry in Wikipedia. (In some cases, Wikipedia articles start with initial contributions by passionate amateurs, followed by contributions from professional scholars/ researchers who weigh in on the "final" versions. Here is where the contested part of the material becomes most usefully evident.) In this open environment, both the content and the process by which it is created are equally visible, thereby enabling a new kind of critical reading—almost a new form of literacy—that invites the reader to join in the consideration of what information is reliable and/or important. (Brown & Adler, 2008)

In similar fashion, some journals in the sciences are practising a new type of openness whereby all reviews and inputs to a published piece are captured as that piece potentially grows and changes shape in response to feedback from readers. No more blind reviews: Authors and readers are exposed to each other. What will be the effect of this level of transparency on the traditionally "closed" world of academe and traditional forms of assessment and evaluation?

The Changing Face of Assessment in the Open World

Sometimes we don't find indications of change where we think we might. A scan of the presentations at a recent international open learning conference, promoting "open education for a multicultural world" (OCW Consortium Global Conference, 2014) uncovered only *one* mention of the word "assessment"—and that was a reference to needs assessment, which is not the type of assessment around which the central issue of assessing open learning pivots. (At this conference, the pedagogical track comprised 24 presentations, but within pedagogy, it appears that no presentation was tackling the very real issue of assessment within open learning. Policy, research and technology, and knowledge dissemination made up the other tracks.)

Nevertheless, the forces outlined in previous sections continue to beat on the walls of the academy. As higher education's online world changes or contemplates change, so also does the nature of assessment within that world. The discussion above identified several global forces within education's purview that demand changes to traditional areas and processes. Some basic tenets regarding assessment and evaluation remain clear: (a) Formal, credential-granting institutions will continue to zealously protect their evaluation turf in the interests of quality and reputation; (b) the trend toward openness and popularization of "voice"—a trend both instigated and fanned by the online world—will continue to find new manifestations in all corners of education; (c) the associated trend of constructivism as a learning approach in Westernized education supports the notion of "voice" and speaks to the interest and value of authenticity—in learning and in assessment.

Given that online learning occurs at a distance, with learners separated from teachers while engaged in learning processes that are mediated through technology, how can viable assessment and evaluation take place? From a constructivist, learner-centred approach, the answer is authenticity. In higher education, authenticity is defined in assessment as "connected to adults' life circumstances, frames of reference, and values" (Wlodkowski, 2008, p. 313) and is prized as a key factor in good evaluation and assessment protocols.

The application of authentic assessment and evaluation strategies to online learning environments can serve as a salient factor in distinguishing face-to-face assessment strategies from distance assessment strategies. While we have previously stated that there should be no philosophical difference in the role of assessment between online and face-to-face environments, the "I can't see you" factor mentioned above is troublesome to many educators. Consider that the most common concern raised about assessment in distance learning is whether or not it permits an increased degree of academic dishonesty. Old, tired tests and quizzes, poorly formatted multiple-choice tests, and "rote" testing techniques—in other words, unauthentic assessment materials that do not ask the learner to relate in a personal or sustained fashion to the material at hand—are more likely to encourage and enable cheating, whether in face-to-face or distance assessment. As Ferriman (2013) points out,

> anyone who wants to cheat is going to find a way to do so, be it for an online course or in a normal classroom setting. While it cannot be completely controlled, you do have some strategies available to you that decrease the likelihood of cheating—or at least discourage it by making life a bit more difficult.

While Ferriman's "making life a bit more difficult" refers to a plethora of technological tools and software designed to oversee computerized test taking, it should also refer to the development of authentic assessment instruments. Of course, a disciplinary difference exists between what is possible and practical in making assessment less fallible. The sciences are more likely to adopt technical solutions to solve issues of academic honesty; the social sciences and humanities will, or should, in more cases, turn to authentic assessments. That said, attempts to automate social sciences and humanities' assessment and evaluation instruments continue, although recent developments by software companies to replicate the "human" touch have been widely criticized for their poor performance and susceptibility to being compromised by savvy learners (Sands, 2014).

UNESCO's 2016 "Advisory Statement" classified academic cheating as *corruption* (Daniel, 2016). In the advisory statement, Sir John Daniel outlined several areas with issues in integrity that, in addition to assessment, included research, credentials, publications, teaching, and higher education in general. Interestingly, the assessment areas highlighted in the report focus largely on traditional assessments, such as tests, and the misconduct that can occur in that type of assessment. There is no mention of authenticity.

Creating Authenticity in Assessment

There are several ways to create authenticity in learning and assessment. Reflecting the meaning of authentic assessment—that which is "connected to adults' life circumstances, frames of reference, and values" (Wlodkowski, 2008, p. 313)—educators can create assessment and evaluation tools that offer learners the opportunity to relate their learning to real-life subjects and real-life problems.

Service learning, for example, offers a type of learning that is located in real-time and is seen by some to provide a solution to perceived weaknesses in today's educational systems (Bok, 2006). Although the opportunities offered by service learning do not specifically cross over to online learning, the philosophy and practice could easily be incorporated into online courses or programs.

Digital badges offer another approach to authentic assessment, one firmly rooted in the online world. The creation and implementation of digital badges as a means of assessment was initiated by Mozilla in 2010 from a likely commercial orientation. However, since that time, in tandem with the many other open initiatives at play in educational *and* private venues, their application to learning continues to gain momentum. As outlined below in a speech by the American Secretary of Education Arne Duncan in 2011, badges can represent engagement, collaboration, and inclusion; in short, badges can reflect authenticity in learning.

> Badges can help engage students in learning, and broaden the avenues for learners of all ages to acquire and demonstrate—as well as document and display—their skills. . . . Badges can help speed the shift from credentials that simply measure seat time, to ones that more accurately measure competency . . . [a]nd badges can help account for formal and informal learning in a variety of settings. (Duncan, 2011)

Mozilla made its initial pitch for badges at the 10th International ePortfolio and Identity conference in London in July 2012. The presentation focused on what Sullivan (2013, p. 1) describes as the "mundane uses" of digital badges as "motivational stickers for engagement and encouragement (such as recognition of signing into a homework help site for 30 days in a row)."[6] However, as she goes on to acknowledge, badges also "have the potential for greater, extended use for individuals in multiple learning environments to create skill and knowledge portraits more comprehensive than a single letter grade or certificate can capture" (p. 2).

The future of digital badges is uncertain, but recent literature reinforces the claim that badges are clearly gaining momentum in learning communities across the globe (Lindstrom & Dyjur, 2017). If badges are gaining momentum and continue to do so, it is because of the transparency of standards—such as date of issue, institution offering the badge, and the demonstration of learning outcomes—to all parties involved in the teaching and learning transaction and because the transparency of standards empowers learners with greater control in displaying their accomplishments digitally and in sharing their professional development with others (Lindstrom & Dyjur, 2017).

The opportunity exists for badges to find their place in postsecondary education and assessment practice because they break learning down into chunks, they require learners to demonstrate mastery of outcomes, and they possess some level of practical usefulness in capturing and reporting that elusive term—lifelong learning. Hensiek et al. (2017) noted in their research that digital badges and assessment guidelines were created and communicated to learners in a hands-on undergraduate chemistry course. In the videos that learners submitted for assessment, students stated their names, showed their face and hands, and then did a task, such as performing a close-up shot of a calibration mark on lab equipment. Mid-semester examinations on how to use the equipment demonstrated that between 74% and 95% of students who received their laboratory badges answered laboratory use questions correctly, and, at the same time, the department saved $3,200 in equipment costs—two very different ways to prove that students had more effectively mastered the learning outcomes of safe and effective use of lab equipment.

---

6 Mozilla's Open Badge representatives Carla Casilli and Doug Belshaw, from the US and the UK, respectively, made the presentation. At the time, the overwhelming response from delegates to the notion was "A great idea . . . but how will it integrate with traditional assessment paradigms?" That is still the question.

What is the lesson here? As the use of digital badges increases, it may become clear when and where they are most effective in influencing student engagement and motivation. Harmon and Copeland (2016) found that students in a public library management course were underwhelmed by the experience of badges and did not plan to pursue them as a form of professional development. This finding confirms that digital badges may not be as effective as a simple "add-on" but may need to be incorporated into deeper and more fundamental changes to instructional design (Stetson-Tiligadas, 2017). Badge taxonomies (McDaniel, 2016) and digital badges possess great synergy with digital game-based learning environments and may contribute to authentic assessment opportunities through these media. Other research suggests badging may be a significant predictor of student self-efficacy and, therefore, learning performance (Yang, Quadir, & Chen, 2016), enabling instructors in online environments to readily identify which students have less self-efficacy and may require greater encouragement.

Casilli and Hickey (2016) put forth two strong arguments indicating that badges might become a more prominent feature on the assessment landscape. The first is that digital badges provide an opportunity for schools to generate more claims of student learning, with more evidence to support those claims. Secondly, digital badges increase the transparency of assessment practice, and through the transparency of badges—which includes metadata, assessments, and artifacts—it is possible that the importance of conventional forms of recording learner performance, for example, transcripts, where there is no supporting evidence of student learning, may diminish. The badge advocates would have us think so, but the only thing we know about the future with certainty is that we are incapable of foreseeing it accurately. However, over time, both educators and those institutions willing to experiment with these bold concepts will move toward developing better badging systems that will be authentically meaningful and acceptable to educators, learners, and prospective employers.

Sullivan too sees the notion of digital badges as "part of this larger and changing learning and assessment ecosystem" (2013, p. 8) that this chapter has labelled the open movement. Emerging concepts of openness and the shift to e-learning in higher education has created a fertile environment for potential synergy between authenticity and assessment.

Concluding Thoughts

The discussion above has ranged across the current state of and trends in the online higher-education world, accessing classic literature in the field in addition to late-breaking developments in several daily online publications. In keeping with the trend of "open" education, as well as with the rapidity of change in a networked world, such sources (for example, the *Chronicle of Higher Education*) are now becoming more acceptable to scholars, in much the same way that Wikipedia has slowly gained some credibility in the academy. On the subject of "open," we cite here Biswas-Diener and Jhangiani (2017), editors of a recent publication on that topic, who wrote in their introduction,

> Open education, open science, open access, and open pedagogy are new phenomena. They are imperfect and many challenges remain to be overcome. However, as the open movement matures and gains momentum, and as the questions it poses grow increasingly nuanced, the boundaries of the movement continue to expand. The open movement represents . . . an optimistic promise for the future as well as a myriad of practical tools and strategies for the present. (p. 6)

But where do we end up with assessment? These things we know for sure: Meaningful assessment and accompanying evaluation are critical parts of the learning cycle. The institution requires, ultimately, evaluation; assessment is also valued for its contribution to the evolution and improvement of learning processes. The transition to more accessible and flexible open and distance, specifically online, learning has given rise to both adapted and innovative assessment and evaluation tools. The "age of open" has challenged and tested traditional beliefs about teaching, learning, and assessment and continues to do so on many fronts.

7 | Planning an Assessment and Evaluation Strategy—Authentically

It is unfortunate, but not infrequent, that instructors throw in assessment and evaluation occasions at the end of their planning process. It's also unfortunate that, often, these activities are designed for purposes *other* than to enrich learning—for example, to provide required measurement data to departments or institutions.

Readers of this book know by now that we support a constructivist approach that views assessment and evaluation, and the tools that frame them, not only as opportunities for interaction among learners and instructors, or between learners, but also for increased growth and learning. To this end, an assessment and evaluation strategy forms an integral part of the course planning process from its inception. We will discuss both assessment and evaluation in this chapter; although our primary focus has been on assessment, and how to create authentic opportunities in which learners can engage, evaluation is usually an imperative in formal learning.

In the learning cycle diagrammed in Chapter 1 (Fig. 1.2), four stages are presented in a circular design. The notion of circularity implies a continuum of never-ending process, a view of design that we support. If we assume that the genesis of a course begins with an idea of content, driven of course by need—"Let's offer a course on the history of music in England in medieval times!"—then attention to assessment and evaluation will follow immediately in and through each succeeding step: outcomes, strategy, and the actual assessment of the course.

Learning Outcomes: Planning for Authenticity in Integrated Learning Environments

Learning outcomes often suffer in reputation, accused of harbouring behaviourist origins or of being reductionist and controlling (Dron, 2007). In more behaviourist-oriented times, a well-written learning outcome was a very lengthy and mechanical item. It comprised three parts: student behaviour, where skills or knowledge acquired were demonstrated through action; conditions of performance, where the circumstances of the learning or action were described (for example, "in an oral presentation"); and performance criteria, where behaviour was compared to a standard, for example, an industry standard.

However, over time, outcomes underpinned by strong behaviourist views have fallen from favour and have evolved into less arduous, less measurement-focused formats that suggest more guidance than measurement, taking on follow-the-roadmap qualities instead of "jump-through-the-hoop" qualities. Eisner's (1994) "expressive outcomes" are designed for accommodating active learning and tacit knowing (Polanyi, 1966; Wenger, 1998) and allow for more creativity and explorative learning than was previously the case following Mager's (1997) model.

Modern-day learning outcomes are enjoying a resurgence of popularity as institutions seek ways to establish their integrity, accountability, and responsibilities to learners. In the United States, several accreditation organizations operate regionally, covering the entire country, examining postsecondary institutions for the existence of learning outcomes, aligned assessment, and integrated curriculum.

The diagram below captures and summarizes much of the material discussed in previous chapters of this book. How do learning outcomes contribute to the realization of deep learning and higher-order, critical thinking?

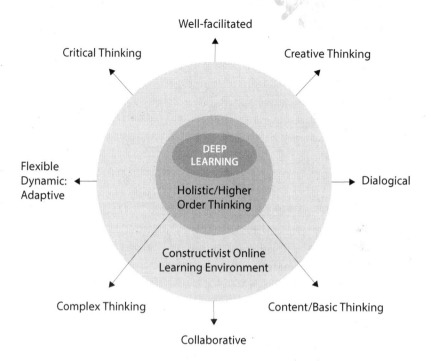

Well-facilitated

Critical Thinking

Creative Thinking

DEEP LEARNING

Holistic/Higher Order Thinking

Flexible Dynamic: Adaptive

Dialogical

Constructivist Online Learning Environment

Complex Thinking

Content/Basic Thinking

Collaborative

Figure 7.1. Deep Learning and Holistic/Higher Order Thinking. An example of an integrated online environment. Source: Morrison, D. (2007).

We consider learning outcomes to be foundational to the construction and evolution of an integrated learning environment. By integrated, we mean that a state of coherence and alignment exists among curriculum parts and that the teaching and learning strategies applied will "use active learning participation and interaction [that will be] facilitative of deep learning and require both higher-order understanding of content and the active construction of knowledge" (Morrison, 2007, p. 107). The initial foray into the teaching and learning dynamic entails a clear delineation of learning outcomes.

Costa and Garmston (as cited in Zimmerman, 2013) developed a model of five levels of learning outcomes that reflect ever-escalating levels of knowledge and potential performance. Ranging far beyond the behaviourist conception of outcomes as rote, basic, technical, or mechanical,

Costa and Garmston's outcomes open the door for authentic performance in cognitive, affective, and social domains.

In ascending order of cognition, expectation and "maturity," their hierarchy of outcomes are described below:

- **Activities.** Activity outcomes ask, "What do I want learners to do?" and "What will learners be doing as they accomplish these outcomes?" The emphasis is on *doing.*

- **Content.** Content outcomes ask, "What concepts or understandings do I want learners to know and how will they show me that they know them?" The emphasis is on *knowing.*

- **Processes.** Process outcomes ask, "What processes do I want learners to develop and how can they show me that they are developing these processes?" The emphasis is on *experiencing,* practising, and "applying cognitive processes. . . to think creatively and critically." (Morrison, 2007, p. 110)

- **Dispositions.** Disposition outcomes ask, "What habits do I want learners to develop and how can I help them in their development? How can they show me that they are developing appropriately?"

- **Mind States.** Mind state outcomes ask, "In which of the five states of mind (efficacy, flexibility, craftsmanship, consciousness, interdependence) do I want learners to become more proficient and how can I help them to become so?" (Zimmerman, 2013, p. 87)

The hierarchy of domains here is clear, as expectations of learners' performance increase from basic "doing," through knowing and applying, to developing the capacity for transferable skills, knowledge, and continued learning (disposition outcomes), and, finally, to mind-state outcomes, representative of the highest order of outcomes that stresses not only cognition but relationships, decision-making, ethics, and authentic behaviour.

Armed with this range of potential learning outcomes, course designers—these may or may not be those who will teach the course—begin to fashion the shape of the course. Working at the outset of the process with the notion of impending assessment, the relevant questions are posed:

- What do I want learners to know?

- What should be evaluated or assessed?

- Why is it important that *that* should be evaluated or assessed?

- What should be discussed? How should it be discussed?

- What approaches/strategies/instruments will provide the best assessment opportunity?

- How will assessment/evaluation instruments or procedures reflect course outcomes?

- When should assessment/evaluation occur?

- How will learners be apprised about upcoming assessments/evaluation?

- What kind of feedback will best benefit learners?

- How/when will that feedback be returned to learners?

Now, let's scrutinize an integrated online environment, as shown in Figure 7.1 above. For the model's components to contribute to the ultimate goal of integrated learning, the breadth and elasticity of learning outcomes, as outlined above, can be brought to bear on the construction of an assessment and evaluation strategy. Morrison (2007), building on the assumption of constructive pedagogy in online teaching and learning, calls for the eradication of the boundaries and siloed thinking that have tolerated the parsing of knowledge into discrete parts that institutional structure (and we, as institutional personnel) handle most easily. For example, institutions tend to box knowledge into courses that perpetuate the myth that knowledge can be neatly separated, assign textbooks as singular sources of knowledge, and fashion departments with some content or disciplinary areas but not others. Regarding learning, Morrison (2007) suggests that "breaking down the barriers between knowledge areas, challenging the concept of disciplines, and creating opportunities for scholars and students to understand the points of intersection between their disciplines" (p. 115) will help us move toward an understanding of knowledge as either a connected whole or a series of parts that are not *un*related.

Many instructors who develop their own courses confuse learning outcomes with topics. With a more accurate understanding of learning outcomes and their potential contribution to both course curriculum and assessment, the stage is set for the appropriate choice and design of course resources and material, interaction, activities, and assessment.

The Assessment Plan

> In developing a course, it is best to begin at the end with the learning outcomes. . . . Being as clear as possible in framing outcomes statements is essential as these will form the basis of student assessment and the overall design of the course, and thus will serve the key goal of fostering deep student learning. (Diamond, 2008, as cited in Ascough, 2011, p. 48)

But where to begin? Despite the skepticism and perceived difficulty around awarding marks to assignments, it remains true that grades are extremely important and motivating to learners (Wlodkowski, 1999). Grades can make the difference between success and failure with the institution and in future studies, work, and life. Their importance cannot be downplayed.

In the "backwards design" sense, following the recommendation of designers to work from the outside in, from the desired end result to the beginning of the learning process, we suggest that assignments that will be evaluated for marks be developed first. These "markers" will serve as guideposts for the subsequent development of activities and other types of formative assessment that will usher learners toward attaining grades.

Developing graded assignments or activities is dependent on the desired outcomes that are driving the shape and rhythm of the course. What are the most important topics? How will you get there—what sequential activities will lead to the most difficult and complex issues? How much time will this take? Are you required by your program or institution to set a final exam? Are you required to allocate a percentage of the total grade to one exam, or to an exam and a midterm test or exam?

Each institution or program will set out its requirements for evaluation. Perhaps you are fortunate enough *not* to have to work within such a designated framework, in which case, with careful consideration, you can construct your own evaluation strategies. The range and variations here are endless, as any search through online syllabi will show. Table 7.1 provides some examples of course syllabi randomly selected from online course offerings:

Table 7.1. Examples of Syllabi for Online Courses.

Course 1: Communications, first year

Stated Outcomes/ Goals	Provide a general history of media and communication technologies, emphasizing their centrality to social, political, cultural and economic life.
	Increase awareness of the importance of mediated communication in daily life.
	Introduce learners to the field of communication studies, with particular emphasis on basic concepts, key terms and theories, as well as its relationship to other disciplines in the humanities and social sciences.
Assessment	Project: 15% (week 6) Mid-term exam: 20% Annotated bibliography and thesis statement: 25% (week 10) Final exam: 25% (end of course) Tutorial participation: 15% (ongoing)

Course 2: Women's studies, second year

Stated Outcomes/ Goals	Understand, paraphrase, and assess key scholarly arguments. Identify and explain factors shaping women's participation in technology based fields.
	Use scholarship to assess popular discussions of gender and technology.
	Explain how gendered metaphors in science and medicine have shaped the development of sexual and reproductive technologies.
	Construct your own coherent arguments about relations between gender and technology.
	Write more clearly and better articulate your thoughts.

Assessment	Critical reflection: 20% (week 7)
	Online discussion: 15% (weeks 4-8)
	Poster presentation: 20% (week 9)
	Flipped classroom activities: 15%, 30% (week 10, week 11)
	Final research paper/project: 30% (end of course)

Course 3: Philosophy, third year

Stated Outcomes/ Goals	Express the basic tenets of major ethical theories and are competent to discuss the strengths and weaknesses of these theories.
	Be familiar with major ethical issues in contemporary bio-ethics and are able to engage critically with material in areas of bioethics.
Assessment	Three timed quizzes, each worth 25% of the final mark, and each consisting of 15 multiple-choice or short answer questions.
	Final assignment consisting of two short essay questions, each worth 12.5% of the final mark.

Course 4: Political science, graduate study

Stated Outcomes/ Goals	Understand how the Canadian health care system works and identify the key policy debates and political issues surrounding the provision of health care.
	Be able to describe various policy options and to analyze the advantages and disadvantages of each.
	Understand the political context underlying these policy alternatives, and to comprehend how political obstacles can undermine constructive policy objectives.
Assessment	Class presentation: 20%
	Policy brief: 30% (week 8)
	Research paper: 30% (end of course)
	Attendance and participation: 20%

Course 5: Education, graduate study

Stated Outcomes/ Goals	Understand the origins of the modern practice of education.
	Craft a well-reasoned personal mission statement referring to the practice of adult education.

Consider thoughtfully the individual and social dimensions of adult learning.

Take a considered position on the philosophy and practices of self-directed learning.

Understand the different views of social learning current in the discipline.

Identify different approaches to emancipatory learning, and make strong arguments for a particular view.

Understand the nature of the learning society and of public pedagogy for our time.

Assessment   Learning journal: 25% (end of course)
Reflective essay: 20% (week 4)
Position paper: 20% (week 9)
Group project: 20% (week 12)
Participation: 15% (ongoing)

Note: These syllabi were randomly selected from Fall term courses in Canadian universities.

As noted throughout this work, our purpose has not been to guide readers in the development of evaluative instruments such as tests and examinations. While we recognize that those types of tools are necessary to determine performance in many situations, we have focused on tools for authentic learning that more often, in the social sciences and humanities, take the form of essays, papers, and projects.

From the material in Table 7.1 above, we cannot presume to understand the rationale for the assessment plan outlined in each course. However, there are a number of questions that should have been, and may have been, asked as these courses and their assessments were being designed.

Course 1: Communications, first year

Project: 15% (week 6); Mid-term exam: 20%; Annotated bibliography and thesis statement: 25% (week 10); Final exam: 25% (end of course); Tutorial participation: 15% (ongoing).

Questions:

- How is the project constructed?
- Is it individually done or group-based?
- What were the parameters of the project regarding topics?
- Did the project topics reflect the content of the first few weeks of the course?
- What are the parameters of the annotated bibliography?
- To what topic/theme do the bibliographic items relate?
- Is this an exercise for research skills or for content-knowledge acquisition?
- Is there an occasion in the course to further use the bibliographic discoveries?
- Why a thesis statement? Is it intended to encompass the research area presented in the bibliography?
- Where does the assessment for analytical and critical thinking skills, as stated in the learning outcomes, occur?

Assumptions:

- The midterm exam will cover material presented to date.
- The final exam will cover either course-wide material or material presented since the midterm.

What if?

- The project was scheduled for later in the course, when learners were more comfortable with each other?
- The bibliography and thesis statement were preparatory to a paper that required both inputs?

Observation

There seems to be no connection between evaluation activities.

Course 2: Women's studies, second year

Critical reflection: 20% (week 7); Online discussion: 15% (weeks 4-8); Poster presentation: 20% (week 9); Flipped classroom activities: 15%, 30% (week 10, week 11); Final research paper/project: 30% (end of course).

Questions:

- Are the poster presentations collaborative or group-based?
- What are the parameters or guidelines for poster topics?
- Do the poster presentations spark online discussion? Debriefing?
- What avenue for discussion and interaction is provided for weeks *other* than weeks 4 to 8?
- What is being evaluated in weeks 10 and 11 during the "flipped" sessions?
- Where are the opportunities for collaboration and exchange?
- What preparation has been made for the large final assignment? Does it build on the poster topic or some aspect of the flipped classroom activities?

What if?

- Learners were provided with a forum for discussion in weeks 1 to 3?
- The flipped classroom activities and final paper/project were integrated in some way?

Observation

Course 2 has a varied assortment of activities that seem well balanced. That nature of the flipped classroom activities is critical, as they occupy four weeks approaching the end of the course. We hope they offer opportunities for discussion, exchange, and interaction.

Course 3: Philosophy, third year

Three timed quizzes, each worth 25% of the final mark, and each consisting of 15 multiple-choice or short answer questions. Final assignment consisting of two short essay questions, each worth 12.5% of the final mark.

Questions:

- How are the quizzes placed within the course? What percentage of content does each "reflect"?

- How inclusive or restrictive are the short essay questions, each worth 12.5%?

- Where is the discussion that is alluded to in the outcomes taking place?

- Where are the learners exposed to the critical engagement with materials alluded to in the outcomes?

- Where do the learners have the opportunity to demonstrate their critical competence?

What if?

- The material being assessed in three timed quizzes was assessed in three short papers that focused intently on the material that the instructor deemed evaluative-worthy?

- One midterm exam substituted for the quizzes—if testing in this way is deemed critical?

- A forum was introduced to permit learners to engage with each other over important course themes or topics?

Observation

Course 3 does not permit, according to the information outlined on the university website, any interaction among learners. It offers no reward or motivation for learners to collaborate or learn creatively with each other. It does not seem constructivist in approach. It appears content-based.

Course 4: Political science, graduate study

Class presentation: 20%; Policy brief: 30% (week 8); Research paper: 30% (end of course); Attendance and participation: 20%.

Questions:

- What is the basis for the class presentation? Individual or group?

- When is the class presentation?

- Does the presentation prepare learners for their major assignments?

- Are presentation topics assigned or chosen? Do they emerge from course topics?

- Is attendance differentiated from participation? How is online "attendance" monitored and evaluated?

Assumptions:

- Both heavily weighted assignments are integral to the intent of the course material as described in course outcomes.

- The higher-than-usual (15% is considered "usual") weight for attendance and participation implies robust opportunities for learner interaction and discussion.

Course 5: Education, graduate study

Learning journal: 25% (end of course); Reflective essay: 20% (week 4); Position paper: 20% (week 9); Group project: 20% (week 12); Participation: 15% (ongoing).

Questions:

- What are the parameters for the group project?

- Are project topics assigned or chosen?

- Why is the learning journal weighted more heavily than the position paper?

- Have learners engaged sufficiently in reflective practices to produce a reflective paper by week 4?

Assumptions:

- The learning journal is an inclusive, course-wide enterprise.

- The learning journal's rubric outlines the need for critical thinking.

What if?

- There was less emphasis on reflective work.

Determining Authenticity and Engagement

How can authenticity be introduced into each of these courses and their assignments? How can engagement among learners be encouraged in order that knowledge can be shared, integrated, elaborated upon, and further built in the constructivist way? Our caveat here is that we have randomly selected these courses as examples; we do not condone the assignment structure in each course. The difference in philosophical approach evidenced by these assignment structures should be apparent to readers. Still, all examples can provide fodder for contemplating the addition of strategies and activities to facilitate more—quantitatively or qualitatively—authentic and engaging learning occasions.

In the communications course, Course 1, almost half the course's grades result from examinations. The project, worth only 15%, is most probably an individual exercise that might afford learners the opportunity to create something authentic—that is, of real-life value to them, of sustained interest, and possibly a topic that could be further developed in the annotated bibliography assignment. Course 1's second learning outcome, "increase awareness of the importance of mediated communication in daily life," opens the door to authenticity for its learners. Aside from the tutorial participation, which no doubt gives learners a chance to bring themselves and their experiences to ongoing discussion and engagement with peers, Course 1 offers no other chance for authentic assessment. While it is possible that on either or both of the course's exams, there are questions that allow learners to analyze, critique, or apply personal experiences in their responses to questions, it is difficult to encourage authenticity in this type of restricted, time-pressured, and directed situation.

Course 2 on women's studies features three outcomes with which learners could authentically engage (the first, third, and fourth). Given this framework, the critical reflection paper which learners produce for week 7 could nicely permit them to enter into an authentic study of the course's themes, perhaps reflecting on their own relationship to technology, to science, or any aspect of gendered relationships in the areas under examination. If the critical reflection paper were designed to build on online discussion topics of weeks 1 to 4, the alignment between assignments and activities would enhance learners' opportunity to build knowledge connections and develop a sustained interest in an area or areas of the course. Likewise, the poster presentation that follows, especially if it were organized as a group activity, could strategically mesh learners and topics in collaborative learning. The same could be hoped from the flipped classroom activities of weeks 10 and 11, although we don't know what they are.

And whether the final assignment is an individual effort or a group effort, it holds the potential to serve as a capstone piece or an expansion of a prior interest. At 30% weighting, the final assignment is also substantial enough to encompass an entirely new topic for exploration and still offer the breadth and depth for a critical or applied study. Course 2 lives up to its outcome expectations in that it gives learners ample opportunity for writing and development, with sufficient time between the two major written assignments for learners to contemplate constructive feedback and apply new learnings to the major project. And although we don't know which activities will represent the flipped classroom in weeks 10 and 11, it's possible that more writing opportunities of lesser intensity are contained in that time period.

The philosophy course, Course 3, appears in its assessment structure to be very traditional and suggests that it has been adapted, without much design, from a face-to-face classroom experience. In that classroom, we surmise, there may have been some discussion between learners and instructor, but it is just as likely that it may have been very lecture-oriented. We do not discern, in this online version, any consideration of constructivist thinking that might be reflected in assignments or activities that offer learners the chance to gather together in knowledge-building occasions. Nor do we see the opportunity for learners to involve themselves deeply in exploring course concepts through prolonged investigation of topics, through group discussion and exchange, or in creative projects. Tests and examinations are more likely to evaluate surface learning rather than the deep learning that constructivist educators strive for (Garrison & Archer, 2000; Hiltz, Shen, & Swan, 2006). With the caution that our observer-eyes cannot know the story of this course with certainty, we feel safe in saying that it offers no opportunity for authentic assessment.

It is customary in graduate work in the social sciences and humanities for assignments to offer learners hearty opportunities to grapple with content: big papers, big projects—assignments that aptly challenge learners to apply their research, organizational, and writing skills to the task. Course 4, a graduate course in political science, reflects a graduate-level format in its assessment plan. However, the content-driven outcomes do not offer or demand, ostensibly, any opportunity for learners to integrate their own experiences with the material. As mature adults (an assumption), and citizens of this or another country, it's reasonable to expect that learners have experiences with the health care system, that they have succeeded or failed within its various purviews, and that they have opinions and historical evidence that could bear on discussions of policy, barriers, and any numbers of "conditions" within the health care system.

Optimally, their experiences will in fact be brought to the table in the discussion forums regardless of the absence of a learning outcome that captures the value or potential contribution of that experience. As an example of the foregoing critique, the second learning outcome, which currently reads, "Be able to describe various policy options and to analyze the advantages and disadvantages of each" could be recast to read: "Be able to describe various policy options and to analyze the advantages and disadvantages of each with reference to the experience of citizens experiencing the health care system."

The fifth and last course chosen for examination is also a graduate course and clearly inspired by constructivist philosophy. Three of the six statement outcomes indicate good potential for learners to engage authentically with course material. Correspondingly, three of the five assignments requiring evaluation appear to accommodate learners' responses to their learning experience(s), present and past. Both the group project (20%) and the discussion forum participation grade (15%) provide opportunities for knowledge-building and collaborative work.

Of these online courses randomly chosen for scrutiny, four out of five stipulate from 15 to 20% for participation in ongoing discussion. It's likely that the discussions are facilitated through a Learning Management System such as Moodle, with its system of forums providing a home for themed and threaded asynchronous discussion. How do learners qualify for participation grades for discussion? How can these discussions foster authenticity? What is the relationship between community and participation?

Community and Participation

Education scholars have amply researched topics pertaining to participation, its parameters, expectations, and protocols (Anderson, 2003; Conrad, 2014; Holmberg, 1986; Kirschner, Strijbos, & Kreijns, 2004; Lee, Srinivasan, Trail, Lewis & Lopez, 2011; Swan, Shen & Hiltz, 2006: Swan, Schenker, Arnold, & Kuo, 2007). The consensus among researchers is that participation is good: it opens the door to critical exchange, when appropriately facilitated; it increases sociability online and, in doing so, for most learners, increases their sense of course satisfaction; and it broadens, "civilizes," and democratizes discourse. Participation also builds trust (Cheng, Nolan, & Macaulay, 2013), which is essential for learning at a distance when learners are not able to make the kinds of visual person-assessment that we have been trained to make since childhood. Participation in the online conversation among learners and instructor also offers an easy foothold for both authentic learning and assessment.

Schwier (2007), in discussing online, interaction-related senses of belonging in terms of metaphor, concluded that, in spite of the complexities of metaphorical language and intent, the notion of "community" was adequate, in fact superior, in describing the online environment. Drawing from Selznick's (1996) discussion of community—which did not arise from a virtual environment but rather a traditional "land-based" environment, Schwier cites his seven elements of communities: history, identity, mutuality, plurality, autonomy, participation, and integration. In updating Selznick's list, Schwier adds his own: an orientation to the future, technology, and learning (2007, p. 69). In the virtual learning environment, the relationship of participation to community might not be so clear. However, research demonstrates that participation by learners in discussion and online activity creates community, and a robust community invites participation (Conrad, 2005, 2002).

Creating and maintaining a sense of community in online learning has been widely acknowledged as critical for learner comfort and affective satisfaction, which are two major factors for success (Akyol, Garrison, & Ozden, 2009; Conrad, 2005; Garrison & Cleveland-Innes, 2005. Rovai, 2002; Rovai & Jordan, 2004; Veletsianos & Navarrete, 2012). Interestingly, in addition to the many academic resources available on this topic, the Internet is rife with "lay" sites from the business, commercial, self-help, and leadership worlds.

It is important to note that online community is different from the Community of Inquiry (CoI). CoI, as discussed in Chapter 1, proposes an inclusive model for the online learning environment, involving three foundational "presences"—teaching, social, and cognitive—and their interaction. It has been discussed that the CoI model and its underlying constructivist philosophy creates fertile ground for implementing collaborative, group, and "deep learning" assessments in higher education. Online community, on the other hand, refers to "a general sense of connection, belonging, and comfort that develops over time among members of a group who share purpose or commitment to a common goal" (Conrad, 2005, p. 1). Community is associated with belonging, safety, trust: a place to gather, exchange, and share.

Scholars of online learning have come to understand how the establishment of a firm sense of community among learners contributes to their learning success and/or satisfaction. We write "and/or" because the two measures are indeed different. That said, community is generally valued for its contribution to both. But how does community figure in to online assessment? Its benefit is no doubt tacitly understood by both online learners and instructors. Spelling it out, as we do here, is akin to explaining that we can stand firmly on solid ground, but we cannot stand firmly on quicksand—a "no-brainer," as some would say.

Garrison, Anderson, and Archer's (2000) CoI model envisions the online learning environment and shows that the anticipated outcomes of that environment are dependent on the integration of its three "presences" in such a way that learners and instructor together create a secure—actually a *closed*—learning environment. This closed learning environment offers not only academic intimacy but also the safety and comfort required for learners to share their stories, knowledge and, in many cases, professional and personal confidences, fears, and hopes. The environment is, quite literally, closed. LMS courses are password-protected so that only registered learners can access the course materials and all discussion therein. Behind the virtual doors of the online course, the sense of community, as defined above, gives learners the confidence to interact comfortably with their colleagues. "Students' comfort with sharing experiences enabled them to be supportive and encouraging of one another as they worked to understand and learn from one another" (Kayler & Weller, p. 140).

Learners' comfort levels are expressed in many ways in online discussion. Anecdotally, many learners have expressed to the authors, both formally (in learning journals) and informally (in email correspondence), the importance of their sense of comfort within the community for their ability and desire to participate, or the opposite. Online instructors can often watch a learner's confidence and comfort level grow as a course proceeds. Online instructors can also watch a learner recede or fade after experiencing some type of negativity online—from a disagreement with another student or an earnest posting that received no take-up from the group; there are any number of circumstances that may cause a learner's comfort level to fall during a course.

In most online courses an evaluative grade is awarded for participation. The reason for this is to encourage observable participation rather than the "lurking" behaviour that many learners have grown accustomed to in large and impersonal face-to-face classes. Active participation is especially expected in online graduate courses, where the analogy is made to sitting around the seminar table engaging in discussion prompted by responses to course materials or to an instructor-led or student-led presentation. How can shy, unsure, or novice learners be encouraged to come forth with their ideas and responses in a medium where there is no hiding? How can confidence be inspired in a medium where the written word is captured, enjoying an archival presence for a considerable length of time?

Building community is the best way—perhaps the only way?—to foster this kind of interaction and participation. The theoretical base underpinning our belief in the value of community has been explored through discussion of the work of Holmberg (1986), Moore (1989), and Garrison and Anderson (2003). In 2004, Kirschner, Strijbos, and Kreijns suggested the "integrated electronic collaborative learning environments" (p. 24) model, for which they defined successful learning environments in terms of tasks: ownership, character, and control. The integration of learners with all domains of the course—including other participants—is critical to the formation of community.

Community is created in various ways and is well described in the literature (Akyol & Garrison, 2008; Bullen, 1998; Conrad, 2005; Eastmond, 1995; Garrison & Anderson, 2003; Harrison & West, 2014; Mayes, 2006). The University of Massachusetts's online teaching handbook, a tidy and useful volume, outlines briefly how to achieve a sense of community within an online group, addressing issues of student-to-student interaction, student-to-faculty interaction, and tone. They suggest creating occasions where students *must* interact with each other, which of course is sensible; however, the "devil is in the details," which in this case includes the nature of task, timing, and tone. We have taken the suggestions in the University of Massachusetts's online teaching handbook (Poe & Stassen, n.d.) and meshed them with our own:

- Limit the size of discussion groups. Smaller groups create a greater sense of safety and encourage more meaningful interaction. However, leaving students to interact in a small group throughout an entire course limits their learning experiences and growth and may also set them up for difficulties if the small group does not coalesce well personality-wise. A better idea is to create a purpose for small-group activities but to maintain the large-group function as well. In a large online group, this formula may have to be modified for logistical reasons.

- Provide an opportunity for students to introduce themselves to the group at the beginning of the semester. This is best handled in an "icebreaker," in an informal way. Make it fun. Ideas include answering questions such as: "Tell us something unique about yourself"; "Where do you live, and why?"; "What is your goal in enrolling in this course?" While creating these kinds of activities for learners, it is important to provide latitude for those who do not want to contribute personal information.

- Establish an informal forum—a "lounge" or a "café"—where learners can share information and resources that might not be directly related to stipulated course activities. As an example, a "Cutest Dog Contest" elicits plentiful light-hearted responses. Those who are not interested do not have to participate.

- Pair each student with a "buddy" in the course to give students a source of support in the online classroom. Students can be matched using a variety of criteria: location, place in program, level of expertise with technology.

- Use learners' names in your responses as instructor to personalize the response, while broadening the response to include all learners. It is important not to reply one-on-one or establish this precedent in online forum postings. The model for online discussion is many-to-many, for pedagogical and logistical reasons. Establish "public-ness," not privacy.

- That said, the climate of safety and trust is enhanced if instructors carefully direct their critical, or sensitive comments to learners privately. Learners should not be embarrassed in the public forum.

- Exercise the utmost in respect and care for each learner. Ask permission before commenting on areas requiring sensitivity (culture, race, politics, etc.). If you plan to use student assignments as examples, seek permission first, and take care to omit any personal references so that the student's identity remains anonymous.

- Encourage learners directly to interact with other learners: "John, based on your insightful comment yesterday about X, can you respond to Allan's question in today's forum?" Ensure when you do this that the learners are competent and able to contribute accordingly.

- Keep your own tone, as instructor, casual and friendly. Help learners fit into this ambience. Many novice learners feel that a sense of formality is necessary to contribute. It is not. Learners come to enjoy a sense of informality; it is easier for them to contribute knowing they will not be held to APA style or required to cite sources. Online discussion is not for essay writing or formal assessment. There are other occasions for learners to demonstrate that they can master academic conventions. Give them the freedom here, in discussion forums, to discuss, explore, and roam, if necessary.

- As an instructor, be accessible and present. Instructor-presence has been shown to be one of, if not *the most*, important factor in successful online courses (Kupczynski, Ice, Weisenmayer, & McCluskey, 2010; Lehman & Conceicao, 2011). Your constant presence aids in creating an atmosphere of shared labour, togetherness, and community.

The increased availability of networking and social media tools in recent years provides more options for creating community online. A 2003 Duke University initiative with iPods demonstrated that digitally native learners easily gravitated to social media for collaborative learning and are comfortable with being technologically linked to the group in a variety of ways (Conrad, 2014). The opportunity for blogs and wikis are now built into many LMSs. YouTube videos are easily mounted in courses. Research has shown Twitter to be a useful, "informalizing" and accessible strategy for creating community (Rohr, Costello, & Hawkins, 2015).

Building and maintaining a cohesive, inviting sense of community among online learners contributes to and fosters their online presence, which in turns permits solid ground upon which instructors can provide ongoing formative assessment during course activities. Each instructor-response post has the potential to highlight important points, critical thinking, insightful ideas, and potential and real connections to other students' thoughts and ideas. Over time and with an appropriate level of confidence, learners themselves will point out the same realizations in each other's work. In this way, the assessment of learners' participation reflects both cognitive ability and engagement.

If the course's opportunities for discussion via seed questions, or whatever stimuli instructors have used, have been pedagogically well constructed, learners' response-posts should also reflect the type of authenticity previously described. That is, they should have been given the opportunity to tackle issues that resonate with their real-life experience:

issues that can have a life over several parts of the course; issues that are current and meaningful; issues that may be ill-defined; and issues that require not a rote or "closed" yes-no response but an appropriate level of critical thought.

Healthy online community contributes in other ways to other types of assessment. Group work is a popular strategy for online learners in that it accomplishes several pedagogical and logistical goals: it provides a venue for learners to work together and share and build knowledge, and it relieves some of the routine of online learning, which can at times become oppressive to learners. Very practically speaking, for instructors, assigning learners to group projects can reduce the evaluation and assessment load considerably.

Online group projects, in our experience, are fairly universally reviled by learners, especially at the outset. There are many valid reasons for learners' distaste for this kind of activity, including those that apply to group projects generally, as outlined in Chapter 5. Learners write consistently in course evaluations and learning journals about group members who do not perform appropriately. Learners often jockey for position within their group and learning styles compete against each other. Logistically, a range of time zones can make synchronous interaction by Skype, telephone, or chat awkward. Still, with proper management, a pleasant ambience, and a sense of community already established within the group, group projects can succeed and provide fruitful learning experiences for their members.

To assist this process, it is recommended that roles be created for group members to fill (Garrison & Archer, 2000; Poe & Stassen, n.d.). Roles, such as "leader," "reporter," "communicator," can either be assigned or negotiated among members. In an adult group, negotiation would be the preferred method. Other suggestions to strengthen the integrity of the group include "taking the group's pulse" from time to time, requesting that the group submit a report on its processes and functioning, and having the group self-assess its performance. Although none of these techniques guarantees a flawless group experience, they can smooth the path. We also suggest that introducing a group project in the last half or last third of a course is preferable to introducing it early on in the course before the class's sense of community has had time to gel. A fuller discussion of group work can be found in Chapter 5.

Online partnerships, role play, and team activities such as debates provide more opportunities in the online classroom for learners to use the positive effects of engaged community to move toward authentic assessments, where "positive" means fulfilling the values of constructivist pedagogy and improving learners' subsequent abilities to build and share knowledge with their colleagues. These activities and their assessments are enhanced through the fostering of community, following the themes outlined below:

- Learners can form partnerships with other learners with whom they feel comfortable or share a situational bond (geographical, familial, cultural) they've been made aware of through informal or formal exchanges;

- Learners will engage more eagerly and consistently in activities that require organizational effort—as compared to solitary activities—when they have some connection with other learners;

- Learners may have a better idea, from previous informal or formal exchanges, of who they can best learn from or collaborate with.

Partnerships or collaborations for further research, study, or work-related ventures can spring out of positively established relationships from online engagement.

Concluding Thoughts

Chapter 7 discussed the hows and whys of planning assessment and evaluation strategies. As emphasized throughout, incorporating the assessment plan into the learning cycle is key to successful learning. Whereas learners' work, produced in whatever format is appropriate, is usually straightforward to grade, the participation issue is more contentious. Participation, exercised in a climate of safe and trusting learning, is connected to the development of online community, and the successful establishment of community in online engagement is essential.

8 | Flexible, Flipped, and Blended

Technology and New Possibilities in Learning and Assessment

This book has, so far, focused on issues of assessment specifically arising from online learning. We have enthusiastically discussed authentic learning and authentic assessment, learner engagement, and how the affordances of online learning and a constructivist philosophy can help to create and implement authentic learning experiences.

Since the advent of computer-assisted learning and Web-based learning, the possibilities arising from the integration of technology with learning continue to grow. Among these possibilities, which will be defined in the sections that follow, blended learning has generated renewed excitement; flexible learning, whose definition is somewhat confusing, represents another "blend" of learning environments; and, more recently, flipped learning has represented a noticeable change in traditional ways of learning. This chapter explores these variations and considers their impact on the shape of authentic and engaging assessment, as we have defined it thus far in this book.

Blended Learning

Blended learning is not new. As far back as 1935, a triad of blackboard, TV, and transmitter was used to reach and teach students outside the classroom (Roscorla, 2014). More recently, Garrison and Vaughan (2008) defined blended learning as "the organic integration of thoughtfully selected and complementary face-to-face and online approaches and technologies" (p. 148). Simply put, this means that some form of blending traditional face-to-face classroom time and activities with online activities will take place. The forms and methods of blending are limitless. Interestingly, this hybrid methodology has brought to the attention of traditional educators the potential of aspects of online teaching and learning for the first time. It may be that their exposure to the power of online learning through blended learning is helping to fuel online learning's rise in popularity and legitimacy. As Rees (2015) recently opined,

> Old style faculty will become dinosaurs whether they deserve to be or not. That's why I recently made a commitment to start teaching online, beginning in the fall of 2016. My plan is to create a rigorous and engaging online U.S. history survey course while I am still in a position to dictate terms. After all, if I create a respectable, popular class *that takes advantage of the Internet to do things that can't be done in person,* then it will be harder for future online courses at my university (or elsewhere for that matter) to fail to live up to that example. (Emphasis added.)

At its most basic level, blended learning seeks to take advantage of the Internet to do things that cannot be done in person. Google Docs, Word-Press blogs, and wikis (inside or outside the LMS) make learning more collaborative and the process of learning more visible to the instructor than ever before. The authors of this book agree with Hill (2016) that online learning has firmly entered the mainstream—despite lingering criticisms from those weighing in on the practice of online learning who lack experience with it. Online learning in contexts that have been well planned and designed with the rigour, engagement, and affordances mentioned by Rees above are especially appreciated by learners. Blended learning is sharing this level of acceptance.

Horn and Staker (2012) claim that the new flexibility offered by blended learning increases the need for formative assessment, which is useful in gauging student progress and guiding the choice of what learning and activities are best to follow. Our view is that the importance of formative assessment has always been there, and that meaningful interaction, engagement, and authenticity among learners have always been integral to active learning, but that the transparency and accessibility of online learning have revealed to new adopters an enormous and previously untapped resource: the learners themselves. Supporting this view, Garrison and Vaughan (2008) stress that blended learning does not simply represent an "add-on" to traditional teaching strategies, but rather that the redesign of teaching and learning that blends technologies with face-to-face encounters creates new possibilities for learning. Garrison and Vaughan call this outcome "multiplicative" (p. 8); they present three notions underlying blended learning: the thoughtful integrating of face-to-face and online learning, the fundamental re-thinking of course design to maximize student engagement, and the restructuring and replacing of traditional class contact hours.

We would argue that blended learning has fuelled (and continues to fuel) a pedagogical renaissance. (We refrain from using the term "revolution.") The heated debates that sought to prove (or disprove) the effectiveness of blended learning or face-to-face learning have led to a deeper exploration of teaching practice, as well a more complex understanding of how students learn. It has been argued by Jensen, Kummer, and Godoy (2015), for example, that the improvements of a flipped classroom may simply be the fruits of active learning. The flipped classroom is a basic blend of activities, where recorded lectures, instructional videos, animations, or other learning objects and resources, are accessed "outside" of class. When students are "inside" the classroom, their online learning experiences are complemented by active pedagogical approaches, such as problem-based learning, case studies, and peer interaction. Blended learning's success has certainly caused fundamental rethinking of course design and what teaching and learning can look like.

In their quasi-experimental study, Jensen, Kummer, and Godoy (2015) looked at unit exams, homework assignments, final exams, and student attitudes to compare non-flipped and flipped sections of a course, and they determined that "the flipped classroom does not result in higher learning gains or better attitudes over the non-flipped classroom *when both utilize an active-learning, constructivist approach*" (emphasis added). The effectiveness of active learning has been established in studies like this and in four major meta-analyses (Freeman et al., 2014; Hake, 1998; Michael, 2006; Prince, 2004) that indicate that the key advantage for blended learning is that it enables students to be active and engaged in various ways, depending on the context and design of the course.

The sought-after result of blended learning is fuller, more resourceful, more integrative learning. For those traditional practitioners whose teaching experiences have been restricted to time-and-place in a bricks-and-mortar environment, the possibilities offered by blended learning are many, and Garrison and Vaughan's (2008) book is a good resource. However, for those practitioners who have already transitioned to online teaching and learning, we imagine (and hope) that the results of such a transition have been achieved through the adoption of a constructivist and engaged *pedagogy* that mixes content attainment with concept application in authentic learning environments.

McElhone (2015) presents yet another lens through which to consider blended learning, based on the question, "*what* are we blending?" She contests the line drawn between physical versus virtual presence and suggests that the notion of "blend" should be opened up to include a smorgasbord of learning activities—formal, informal, Web-based, people-centred. Although her corporate background prompts her to include, as strategies, webinars and online modules as "training" applications, she also focuses on relationships (mentoring, feedback, and collaboration) and real-life applications (practical and applied assessment) in order to make learning better. Elsewhere, Roscorla (2014), investigating the excitement around blended learning, suggests that perhaps it will expedite learner completion and success. On that note, prior learning assessment (see Chapter 5) has also been presented as a route to faster completion, which is one of its most obvious attractions to learners.

What blended learning has done, most of all, is cause a fundamental rethinking of learning-as-delivery and of content as an item for mechanistic transfer. It has also refocused discussion on how to design learning environments so that students are offered the best opportunities for engaging at a deep level with the content and with others in the learning environment. As Feldstein and Hill (2016) observe, when "content broadcast" (content attainment) is moved out of the classroom, it provides more space to "allow the teacher to observe the students' work in digital products, so there is more room to coach students" (p. 26) in the concept-application phase of learning.

We are concerned here only with the intersection of blended learning and assessment, and we find ourselves landing squarely back on the concept of authenticity—the creation of meaningful real-life opportunities with which learners can enthusiastically engage. We have described, in prior chapters, authenticity and its place in assessment and the teaching-learning dynamic. However blended-learning design is to be incorporated into teaching and learning, the relationship of authenticity to assessment, and vice versa, does not change. To the constructivist, that meld is still *the* answer.

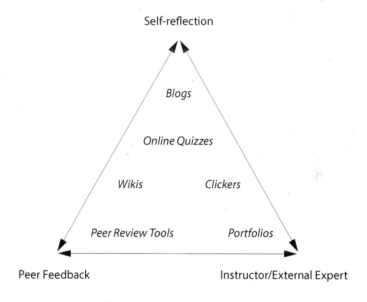

Figure 8.1. A Triad Approach to Assessment. The Community of Inquiry's use of digital technologies to support a triad approach to assessment. Source: Vaughan, N. D., Cleveland-Innes, M., & Garrison, D. R. (2013, pp. 94-95).

To this end, we consider the well-known Community of Inquiry (CoI) model, which developed a triad approach to assessment while also providing a model for planning assessments by identifying the most beneficial technologies and interactive platforms to use. Like Webb and Gibson (2015) and Herrington, Oliver, and Reeves. (2006), the CoI model suggests that digital technologies can provide fertile ground for assessing higher-order skills, supporting interactions, and generating synergies among learners and instructors. From a blended learning-advocacy stance, the triad model reiterates and supports the strengths of online learning, where technology becomes "an enabler for increasing meaningful personal contact" (Feldstein & Hill, 2016).

The triad approach highlights several technological tools that can be used for self-, peer-, and instructor-led assessments. Below are some examples of how these tools have been used to create dynamic and robust assessment approaches.

"Clickers"

Student response systems (SRS, aka clickers) offer a powerful and flexible tool for teaching and learning. They can be used peripherally or they can take a central role during class, but even with minimal use, significant differences have been found in final grades between sections of the same course (Caldwell, 2007; Lantz, 2010). In our experience, clickers can be used to increase student participation, integrate with other commercially provided learning resources to provide useful feedback to instructors on student learning, and increase opportunities for fun through formative assessment practices. In a small community college, instructors used clickers in various ways, including using them for comprehensive review at the end of a module, or for students to "get their head in the game" and activate prior learning at the beginning of class with 5 to 10 short questions. Other instructors used them with icebreaker activities to solicit student opinions on controversial topics to which they might be reluctant to admit without the veil of anonymity, as a way to launch discussion. Others used it for team-based games where students competed for top points. Students enjoyed the increased interactivity and faculty felt more able to assess the learning of the entire class rather than random, individual students. Based on student content attainment, faculty developed remedial lectures on specific elements and were able to reflect on whether or not their instructional approaches were successful. Through think-pair-share (or teach-test-reteach), the opportunities for peer instruction—where students teach each other concepts through discussion—are endless. The relevance of clicker use to blended learning centres on its ability to create dynamic interaction and assessment potential among learners in the classroom-based part of the "blend."

Wikis

Wikis can be used to assist in group assessment. Group assessment, as was discussed in Chapter 5, is fraught with difficulties. Group assessment is often necessary because of the massification and "scalability" of higher education, where some undergraduate courses have upward of 1,000 students. In a pedagogical sense, group assessment has become popular because the collaborative nature of the assessment task provides the opportunity for learners to develop interpersonal skills such as leadership and communication.

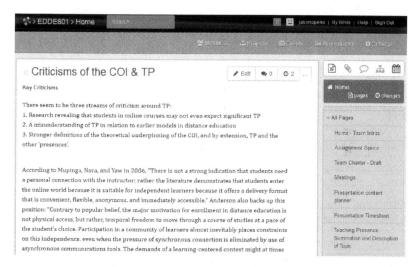

Figure 8.2. An example of a group wiki from Athabasca University's EdD program.

Wikis enable group collaboration, but they also afford the instructor the ability to track individual participation and contributions. Eddy and Lawrence (2013) suggest that wikis are excellent as platforms for authentic assessment because they are a user-friendly Web space that supports collaborative authorship and learner choice; they also meet the calls for authenticity and accountability by allowing students to focus on "real world tasks." Wikis are a flexible tool when crafting assessment tasks. They provide a way to document student learning because they reduce the limits and time constraints of collaboration while promoting a fundamental rethinking of what it means to be "face-to-face" and "in the classroom."

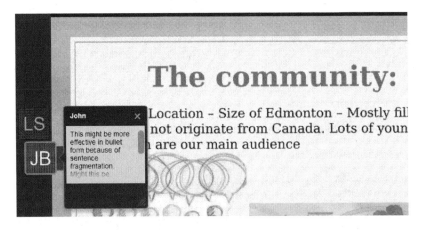

Figure 8.3. Peer Review Tools. Peer review tools, such as VoiceThread, enable learners to engage with grading criteria and revise their products based on peer feedback.

Blogs

The term "blog" was coined in the late 1990s (as a short form of "weblog"), and blogs are now one of the older forms of user-generated content. Blogs are so "old school" that they have given way to other social media platforms, such as Twitter (micro-blogging). On this topic, the popular blogger Seth Godin (2016) has suggested that Google and Facebook no longer want people to read blogs because they are free, uncensored, and exist outside their walled gardens. Still, blogs remain an effective strategy as a form of student engagement to foster collective and reflective learning (Mansouri & Piki, 2016). While students primarily use blogs for entertainment and personal fulfillment, it has been suggested that "we would be more effective teachers if we helped students solve their real-world personal, professional, and academic writing problems by building on existing practices, including the flexible use of the composing technologies that permeate their everyday lives" (Moore et al., 2016). Blogging offers a powerful option for formative assessment, whether it takes place within the closed environment of the LMS or out on the open Web as a way to facilitate collaborative learning, reflection, and social support. As Garrison and Akyol (2009) suggest, this venerable Web 2.0 tool goes beyond simple interaction, giving learners the opportunity to engage in purposeful discourse to construct meaning, share meaning, and consolidate understanding at both personal and conceptual levels. Blogs may produce the greatest benefits for students who are shy, introverted, or naturally reflective (Ciampa & Gallagher, 2015).

This brief look at clickers, wikis, and blogs highlights the dynamic and flexible digital tools that can be used to create sophisticated blended-learning environments. Such environments enable faculty and learners to engage with, critically monitor, and assess the quality of learning taking place in any form of educational provision. These standard tools are now being complemented by other social networks, such as Twitter, to expand assessment approaches. Twitter has been used to enhance social presence in large-enrolment online courses (Junco, Heiberger, & Loken, 2011; Rohr & Costello, 2015; Rohr, Costello, & Hawkins, 2015) or to increase concept retention, course enjoyment, and student achievement by creating avenues for student engagement that supersede those available via traditional classroom activities. Others (Barnard, 2016) have taken advantage of Twitter's strict character limit to teach creative writing and storytelling skills. As mentioned earlier, the affordances of these tools provide limitless opportunities to construct more creative assessment approaches.

Flexible Learning

Flexible learning is a generous, convenient label for the many blends of learning affordances now available thanks to infusions of technology over recent years. The key to optimizing the use of such flexibility is understanding its myriad dimensions and contributing factors. Issues and factors to be considered in making course design decisions include the following:

- the "anytime, anywhere, anyhow" element
- appropriate application of technology and delivery mode
- appropriate choice of pedagogy—instructional approaches, resources
- timing, logistics, organization

But what about assessment? Several resources on flexible learning that we accessed for research on this topic—from universities, governments, and private enterprise—did not mention assessment at all. Burge, Gibson, and Gibson's (2011) edited volume on flexible learning did not mention assessment, while their concluding chapter re-emphasized the pervasive institutional issues with which we are all familiar: resistance to change, change dynamics, organizational structure and policy, costs, and "false promises and false prophets" (p. 336). Quite possibly, this predictable absence is because the need to assess learning competently remains the same; the need *always* remains the same. However, putting assessment into practice often yields a wide range of strategies and instruments.

In their discussion of flexibility in distance learning and through their critical examination of the "goodness" that flexible learning connotes, Burge et al. (2011) emphasized the potential of technology, the many different flexibility advantages, the learner-centredness of flexible learning, and the opportunity for the variety of strategies that it allows. Flexible-learning approaches can, theoretically, lead to greater authenticity and engagement for learners. Whether these promises are fulfilled is dependent upon factors both individual and institutional, as we have discussed in previous chapters in this book. On its own, flexible learning holds no guarantees.

One of the most promising aspects of flexible learning and assessment is contained within the concept of differentiated assessment: "An educational structure that seeks to address differences among students by providing flexibility in the levels of knowledge acquisition, skills development, and types of assessment undertaken by students" (Varsavsky & Rayner, 2013, p.790), rather than taking the "middle of the cohort teaching approach." There are significant challenges and opportunities in giving students choice for how they will provide evidence of learning. Again, massification, scalability, reduced funding, or developing rubrics that can be fairly and meaningfully applied in a high-choice, high-variability environment are all significant challenges. However, differentiated approaches to assessment in higher education potentially provide a genuine framework for student learning because they recognize that learning is, by its very nature, an individual experience (Varsavsky & Rayner, 2013).

Differentiated assessment also reflects sound adult learning principles, such as giving students—particularly adult students—control over how they will be assessed. By allowing participation in the creation of their assessment, learners become co-creative participants in their experience, affording them the opportunity to generate ideas about what would be the most meaningful, valuable, and hands-on ways to demonstrate their learning.

The Flipped Classroom

The recent flipped classroom phenomenon is a subset of flexible learning. Based on constructivist principles, the flipped classroom allocates the "delivery" of material to home-time, using computer-based instructional methods, and reserves precious face-to-face classroom time for interactive activities such as discussion, presentations, debates, group work, and role play. In this way, learners presumably come to class forearmed with the knowledge required to participate in engaging activities that are both more authentic and more interesting than the lecture-style classroom. Brame (2013) posits that the flipped classroom permits Bloom's lower levels of cognition to occur outside of class while the higher levels of cognition, such as creativity, are practised within the classroom and the group environment. The flipped classroom presents interesting assessment opportunities that, while not new in themselves, could potentially expand the application and usage of authentic assessments.

Flipping the classroom permits, theoretically, learners to come to learning activities prepared to engage. Speaking cynically, one could say that such situations would resemble a mature learning environment where learners are present by choice, well prepared, and eager to participate. Cynicism aside, with prepared and eager learners, a flipped classroom provides opportunities for authentic and engaging assessment.

Out-of-Classroom Preparation

As with any "seek and find" or research activity, out-of-classroom prep-aration is more exciting than sitting in the lecture hall. That learners can connect with each other using Web-based technologies increases the potential for collaboration, community, camaraderie, and excitement. It allows for design activities that, while do-able, are challenging and fun. As always, the type and level of activity will depend on the learners, on their maturity and readiness levels. Novice learners require more guidance on activities and generally access a lower cognitive level on Bloom's Taxonomy (1956), while more advanced or mature learners can more easily engage in activities that require higher level skills, such as synthesis, evaluation, or creativity. Some activities that engage learners while they prepare their out-of-classroom materials might include treas-ure hunts, contests, dyad or paired-activity, self-quizzes, worksheets, preparation of a document that records cognitive process such as a mind map, or a small media presentation using any one of the software products freely available.

Should this work be graded? The decision to award grades for a piece of work in a course is tied to the learning cycle, to the materials under discussion, and to the fit of those materials and that topic into the course design. Given these factors, there is no one-size-fits-all answer to this question. That said, a course-wide participation grade could contain marks for completing at-home preparation successfully. On a broader scale, a larger assignment, perhaps spread over a longer period of time, could stand alone as a graded activity. Whatever the choice, instructors must ensure that their grading or weighting scheme is fair to learners, especially if they are preparing the work "cold," without any previous exposure to the topic, and prior to arriving at the in-class session.

While pre-class tests to measure the degree of preparation that occurred outside the classroom are suggested in some literature (Bishop & Verlager, 2013), adult educators do not favour tests for their mature students; if a testing occasion is warranted, a self-quiz is preferred.

In the Flipped Classroom

Once the prepared learners are in the face-to-face classroom, time can be spent in active engagement, learners-with-learners. Apart from perhaps an initial "consolidation of learning" period that could be conducted in small groups, with large-group reporting, or as a large group, the instructor is freed from lecturing or otherwise presenting the material. In-class activities can now "focus on higher level learning objectives" (Brame, 2013). Learners can engage with the teacher and each other in applying their new knowledge or moving further, with the teacher's encouragement and guidance, in their understanding of it (Reigeluth, 2012). During class time, small group discussion can work to promote deeper understanding; guided large-group discussion can achieve the same results. The keys to successful in-class activity are interaction and the application and synthesis of knowledge.

Assessment, from this point on, will take on whatever instruments best suit the learning design to achieve intended outcomes. The variety of assessments in the flipped classroom arises from the out-of-classroom portion of the class and are plentiful, and learners' responses to flipping the classroom have been positive (Bishop & Verlager, 2013). Our own experience confirms this positive response. In an ongoing research project at a small community college, when students were interviewed about the benefits of a flipped classroom environment, they responded positively to the sense of control they felt they had in the instruction process (Openo, 2017). They studied in the kitchen, in cafés, or on their beds. With video, they could rewind (or fast-forward) parts of the lecture or re-watch sections they were unclear of. They had time to process, reflect, and develop more meaningful questions. They also had control over their energy. As one student put it, "In [a] lecture, by the end of class, I didn't want to ask questions because I just want to get out of there, and I know I didn't absorb half of it because I'm tired." But with the flipped classroom, "I can do it when I know I am going to be able to focus." This is a perfect expression of what Anderson (2004) calls temporal freedom, and if students can interact with lectures multiple times and at times when they feel ready for learning, this affordance will likely be evidenced in their assessments.

Social Media

We have alluded to social media and its contributions to online learning throughout this book. There is no denying the power and influence of the inclusion of social media in its many forms. Twitter, YouTube, blogs, wiki: all contribute to increased connectivity among learners, flexibility of modality, and, perhaps we can assume, renewed vitality. Social media enhances the distribution and sharing of ideas and opinions, material, resources, and experiences. It's a brave new connected, colourful, and vibrant learning world!

What does such innovation mean for assessment in the social media–rich learning environment? We would suggest, at the heart of it, in the most basic and pedagogical sense, nothing. It is worth quoting Salmon's unvarnished and economical adage: "Don't ask what the technology can do for you, rather [ask] what the pedagogy needs" (cited in JISC, 2010, p. 16). Our stance does not seek to diminish the contributions of social media, nor does it deny the fact that many new doors and windows have been opened for learners. Rather, we maintain that the essence of assessment does not change: Whatever the medium and regardless of the reasons, assessment and evaluation *exist* and will likely continue to do so.

Paulin and Gilbert (2016), in their chapter on social media and learning in the new *Sage Handbook of E-Learning Research*, approached the issue of assessment but didn't quite land on it. In fairness, it may be that they didn't intend to, as the word assessment is not used, but rather the words *measuring* and *measurement* are. Perhaps the issue in their approach lies in this sentence: "Since learning through social media transcends the boundaries of traditional learning platforms and environments, it can be difficult to measure if and how students learn in these environments" (p. 362). Did the measurement of learning change when blackboards became whiteboards? When videoconferencing tried to replace audio-teleconferencing? It did not. The notion of assessing or evaluating learners' handling of material and experiences presented to them has remained constant. But yes, the nature and type of potential assessment and evaluation instruments, tools, and processes has evolved and grown.

Where we once had just paper, we now have many types of computer-based and computer-generated assessment tools. (As we pointed out in the Preface, these tools were not intended to be a topic in this book.) Where learners once toiled with pens to write on that paper, they can now rap out their work on their computers and upload the results to a course dropbox. More creatively, they can create a Powtoon cartoon or a Prezi display. Their instructors can enter their comments on their documents, on their slides, on their animations, or use voice technology. The variety of possibilities is vast and, most would agree, wonderful. But that's just the technology of social media learning; Salmon, as well as all constructivist researchers and these writers, would have you consider the pedagogy.

In his book on constraint and control in online learning, Dron (2007) deftly analyzes the impact of social software on the structure and dynamics of online learning from a theoretical and design point of view. While he doesn't address the issue of assessment, some of his observations and conclusions can provide a foundation for that discussion. For example, Clay Shirky's first definition of social software is "software that treats groups as first-class objects in the system" (as cited in Allen, 2004). This is a useful definition for our work on assessment, as it implies the issue of agency in the structure-agency relationship.

Clarifying the meanings of "social software" and "social media" is difficult even for those technologists who work in this field (INCLUSO, n.d.). The INCLUSO (Social Software for the Social Inclusion of Marginalised Youngsters) manual suggests that social media is a more up-to-date term than social software, but points out that, at the end of the day, we are still referring to a set of tools: "Tools like email and message boards are decades old. . . today these tools are supplemented by such software as blogs, chat and social network(ing) sites." We would like to add this nuance to the separation of the two terms: The term social media adds a dimension of agency, because "media" implies active use of tools, whereas "social software" implies structure, because "software" is just that—structure. Shirky's (2009) emphasis on the importance of groups supports the notion of agency.

Correspondingly, Dron (2007) notes the difficulty in controlling "effective and coherent sequence[s]" (p. 295) in learning environments based on social software. In other words, in a McLuhanesque fashion, the user is becoming the message. In his list presenting the "argument of this book in 10 stages" (p. 311), Dron's numbers 8 and 10 speak effectively to a discussion of assessment:

> 8. In some senses, social software allows learners to engage in a form of dialogue as well as to benefit from the resulting structure, thereby providing both high and low transactional distance not at the same time, but under the continuous control of the learners.

> 10. In such an environment, the self-organising feedback loop derived from the collective intelligence of its inhabitants offers the potential for a qualitatively different and (probably) better learning experience.

Dron is emphasizing the key importance of learners as agents of their own learning and placing into their hands the potential for self-direction and organization within an online learning experience. This concept supports the provision of assessment vehicles that encourage, permit, and capture the energy generated by the "collective intelligence" and autonomy of the group. Taken together, this is a strong endorsement for constructivism and authentic assessment.

The tools and the theory are in place for informed instructors to not only support constructive knowledge-building efforts but also to provide creative assessments. We have discussed and described what some of those assessment instruments can look like throughout this book.

To recap briefly, we have provided some suggested activities for assessment that make use of social media.

Project Work

Undertaken individually or in groups, setting learners loose on a relevant topic with well-defined guidelines and criteria will yield creative results. Encourage the use of social media tools but caution learners not to lose themselves in technology. Guidelines should provide instruction on how to stay on task. As a guard against the illicit "borrowing" of material from or the wholesale import of an OER, ensure that the project topic is closely tied to course themes or directions and include requisite nods to learners' individual experiences or practices in the field.

Trawling the Internet

We all hunt through the Internet for our resources, whether it be writing a student paper or writing a book. How many of us remember those afternoons spent in the university library thumbing through endless index cards? With a clearly outlined task and appropriate guidelines, send learners on a directed quest to satisfy a question, a challenge, a chronology, a debate—whatever is most appropriate and pedagogically complete. Specify that sources be meticulously recorded.

Critiquing the Internet

Encourage learners' critical thinking skills by creating the modern-day equivalent of a bibliography or article-review. In addition to locating and critiquing topic-relevant material, learners will experience the range of quality—and non-quality—of Internet resources. A group-based, guided debrief on the results can provide another opportunity for the use of software tools.

Blogs

Many of your learners are already accomplished bloggers. Create opportunities for them to apply their blogging skills to an assignment for private, class-only viewing—or not. Some will detect a delicacy here around learner-generated "public pedagogy" and the wisdom of its use. Are your learners ready to go live with their efforts and conclusions? These questions require individual attention from the instructor depending on situation and circumstance. For further discussion on the related topics of peer-assessment and self-assessment, see Chapters 6 and 9. (When using blogs for either summative or formative assessment, ensure that you can access the blog without extensive password control. Over time, needing password permission can become very labour intensive. Also ensure that you can easily engage with the blog to include your feedback or commentary.)

Role Play and Simulations

In traditional classrooms, it was easy to stage a role play as a learning experience or assignment. However, online role play, before the advent of social media, was reduced to the use of somewhat tedious scripts and text. The value of role play has blossomed with the new tools available, as learners can enhance their roles with animation, video clips, avatars, and Second Life, to name a few. As always, there will be learners who are so technologically proficient and keen that it is easy for them to forget the pedagogical intent of the assignment. Keep this front and centre with careful instructions and an appropriate grading scheme.

Assessing Social Media–Based Assignments

Grading assignments that are completed using social media raises new issues. Social media, as outlined above, open the door to much more variety and creativity than was possible on paper. In a similar fashion, the criteria used to grade in the past demands an update. While it is possible to continue to award points for content and mechanics, it's really no longer sufficient. Word length? Page length? In most social media instances, these criteria are no longer relevant. Some possible grading criteria are suggested below.

Content

In most cases, content should continue to be a primary focus for learners. Achieving some level of mastery of required content remains a basic premise of learning and assessment.

Mechanics

At university level, the need to express yourself clearly and articulately is key. We suggest, however, that there are certain places in social-media–based assignments where an emphasis on mechanics is less important than the message or content of the presentation. In role play, for example, when an avatar or character is "in character," mechanics could be dismissed in the quest for authenticity. Similarly, in an informally constructed blog designed to capture in-the-moment inspiration, the emphasis on grammar and sentence structure could be decreased or even omitted. As always, the criteria for grading should be made explicit.

Choice of Medium

In a media world full of choice, should the choice of medium constitute a factor in the grade? Does an animated cartoon presentation carry the message more effectively than a PowerPoint presentation? Is audience participation or enthusiasm a factor? If feedback or response or follow-up is a part of the project, perhaps it is. These decisions are as important for instructors—in choosing a designated medium or a range of choices as vehicles for presentation—as they are to learners.

Creativity

Choice of medium could be included in the broader criterion of creativity. If the course is not a course in communication or design, should creativity matter? Again, consider the purpose of the assignment. Is it intended to evoke the interest and participation of others? Does the knowledge sharing and knowledge building among members that may result from the project hinge on "pulling them in?" Sometimes, we have seen the notion of creativity slightly disguised as "audience participation." Often, in these instances, participation from the group is also measured in terms of the interest sparked and the quality of response to the presentation or topic. Although this appears to be a valid criterion for assessment, grading learners' creativity remains a murky area. Whatever the case, criteria guidelines should be clearly defined.

A Feedback Loop

In certain subjects or areas of learning, reflective thinking is more prized and valuable than in others. In the humanities and social sciences, areas that we have focused on in this book, there are many opportunities to encourage this important skill. As a part of the assessment activities, and falling into the purview of self-assessment or peer-assessment, learners might reflect upon the experience of having done what they've done, having presented what they've presented, having moderated what they've moderated or facilitated online, and so on. Again, this is Schön's (1983) reflection-on-action in action, giving the learner the opportunity to sit back and think about the experience that has just passed. While the grading of such an activity often presents another area of contention, these writers believe that with careful instruction, these reflections can be valid occasions for evaluation, especially since they follow on the heels of, and relate to, a presentation or document that has already been reviewed. That said, the grade weight of such a piece should be kept low and may be perceived to be not worth the effort for either learners or instructor.

The New Normal?

Guri-Rosenblit (2014) points out that "one of the main conclusions of the OECD [Organization for Economic Cooperation and Development, 2005] study was that most higher education institutions use online teaching *to enhance classroom encounters rather than to adopt a distance teaching pedagogy*" (p. 109, emphasis added). She concluded that the historically clear and distinct functions of distance education providers were no longer clear and distinct; we now see that any bricks-and-mortar institution can extend itself to students outside its on-site campus and offer online courses in some format to learners. Has this become the "new normal" over the past decade, since the OECD study? As more and more "blended learning" research is undertaken, its implementation appears to be comfortably embedded within online global teaching practice.

As far back as 2006, researchers at Educause's Center for Applied Research (Albrecht, 2006) wrote that,

> the battles over the efficacy of residential learning versus online learning have disappeared with the quiet adoption of blended learning. While an occasional attack surfaces, the attraction of mixed delivery mechanisms has led to implementation, often without transcripting and virtually without announcement. (p. 2)

Looking to the future, we echo Moebs' (2013) conclusion that,

> blended learning combines mobile learning and (flipped) classroom sessions. The terms m-learning, e-learning, and blended learning have disappeared. People are learning with whatever device is available and the learning systems are flexible enough to allow everybody to start at the appropriate level. (p. 52)

Similarly, Ontario's distance education consortium, Contact North (2012), when looking at the long-term strategic perspectives among Ontario college and university presidents, suggests that blended learning works because it is evolving naturally, because students like and demand it, and because faculty members find that it enhances, rather than replaces, their traditional teaching methods. In fact, Contact North suggests that "it is highly likely that such terms as 'online,' 'hybrid,' or 'blended' learning will disappear in the near future as the technology becomes so integrated into teaching and learning that it is taken for granted" (p. 10).

Concluding Thoughts

For those already engaged in fully online teaching and learning, the recently heralded innovations of blending and flipping do not bring much to the table. We have already adjusted to and accommodated distributed learning and all that it means in terms of interaction, activity, engagement, and assessment. Having celebrated the arrival of techniques that can be helpful stepping stones for traditional classroom educators, our literature is now breaking down label-barriers and embracing a mash-up of learning approaches utilizing wikis, blogs, Twitter, and differentiated assessment. Flexibility is key. Assessment, as already noted, is a critically important, vital part of the learning cycle. Instructors and instructional designers need to be clear about the assessment choices they make; do they align with the learning outcomes and one's teaching philosophy? Is the choice of an essay, a portfolio, a wiki or a blog the most appropriate assessment method? Do these affordances enable increasingly meaningful personal and interpersonal contact, or greater learner choice and control? Are they selected to reduce grading loads, which is deemed by many to be a perfectly reasonable factor upon which to make an assessment decision? While there is no recipe for the perfect blend, these considerations are necessary as one rethinks assessment strategies in a blended learning environment.

9 | A Few Words on Self-Assessment

There are three things extremely hard: steel, a diamond, and to know one's self.

—Benjamin Franklin, *Poor Richard's Improved Almanack* (1750)

We have discussed many types of collaborative activities and their potential for authentic assessment, including online partnerships, team activities, and the creating of community. Does self-assessment offer a competing stance? What is its value to learning?

Fenwick and Parsons (2009) define self-assessment as "the act of identifying standards or criteria and applying them to one's own work, and then making a judgment as to whether—or how well—you have met them" (p. 111). In their discussion of self-assessment, they point out that many learners resist engaging in self-assessment: It makes them nervous; they are uncomfortable; they don't feel they have the skills. Dron (2007) suggests another negative outcome or perception of self-assessment when he writes that assessing one's own work lessens the effectiveness of "communicating [one's] success to others" (p. 102).

Self-assessment cannot occur in a vacuum; that is, well-intentioned instructors should not just throw a self-assessment activity into the mix and hope for meaningful results. From a constructivist perspective, self-assessment represents a step on the path to critical reflection and growth, to independence in learning and self-direction (Garrison & Archer, 2000). The opportunity to self-assess, properly managed, can increase the ability to reflect; the ability to interact—with self, instructor, and colleagues; the ability to think critically and diagnose both weaknesses and strengths in one's own work; and the ability to analyze, synthesize, and of course evaluate. These are all high-level cognitive skills according to Bloom's *Taxonomy of Educational Objectives* (1956). This chapter first discusses some techniques and strategies for introducing self-assessment, then locates self-assessment within the online context, and finally draws on the literature to appraise the use of self-assessments.

Some Tips for Self-Assessment

As self-assessment is a facet of the constructivist approach to teaching, the assumption in this chapter is that the learning environment is constructivist-friendly: Learners are engaged with the instructor, the material, and each other in respectful and participative ways, and opportunities are provided for knowledge building and knowledge sharing (Bereiter & Scardamalia, 1987). Feedback is frequent, formative, and constructive.

In such an environment, critical thinking and reflection are prized. Among the many opportunities that learners would have to practise these skills, individually and in groups, is the chance to self-assess. Garrison and Archer (2000) see self-assessment as a chance for learners to think and write about their own work and their learning; they separate it from "the evaluation of outcomes" (p. 168), which they deem "more formal." The issue of learners awarding themselves grades generates self-assessment's underlying contentiousness, and it echoes, conceptually, Dron's concern about the value of the grade awarded: It depends on who gives it. Similarly, Garrison and Archer suggest that the use of self-assessment—and peer assessment—be approached with caution. They also warn that neither should replace the use of more formal evaluations, conducted by the instructor.

Nevertheless, self-assessment can still serve as a useful learning strategy. Fenwick and Parsons (2009) list these ways to introduce and encourage self-assessment:

- Be aware of learners' sense of power dynamics in the teaching-learning or institution-learning relationship and of the tendency for possible initial reluctance or fear when asked to self-assess.

- Ensure that your plan for self-assessment has a legitimate and logical place within your overall assessment plan.

- Inform the learners of the self-assessment intent, strategy, rationale, and general plan.

- Create and provide clear guidelines and criteria for the self-assessment activity.

- Work collaboratively with learners and help them to work collaboratively with each other, to develop appropriate skills for the tasks.

- Be present to give feedback and support.

- Provide opportunities for debriefing and processing of the development and implementation process. (pp. 113–115)

The Features of Online Self-Assessment

Using self-assessment techniques online falls well within the guidelines and initiatives for authentic assessment already discussed in previous chapters, specifically Chapter 4. These guidelines and initiatives support the notions of motivated, mature, and "deep" learning that flow from constructivist adult education principles. Additionally, online systems make "peer and self-assessment achievable anytime, anywhere" (JISC, 2010, p. 43).

The engagement of learners in self-assessment tasks does not differ from learners' engagement in other online tasks: They are able to complete the task in their own space and, within the confines of the course plan, at their own pace and time. The time-frame assigned to self-assessment activities should reflect a critical-thinking type of task; in other words, it should not be a timed quiz.

Reflective exercises such as logs, diaries, or journals can serve as self-assessment activities in that they encourage learners to assess how well they've met the assessment criteria in other, more traditional tasks such as essays and presentations. The University of Reading, in the United Kingdom, also suggests that "audits or essay feedback questionnaires that students complete on submitting a piece of coursework are particularly helpful as [instructors] can compare [their] perception of their work with students' views on how well they have performed" (n.d.).

To fully realize the potential of self-assessment, as it is understood by educators such as Garrison and Archer (2000) and Dron (2007), it is essential for learners to be given the opportunity to debrief the exercise. Opportunities such as this, provided to assist learners in self-reflection and critical thinking, require reporting and discussion on the processes undertaken. Some of the questions that could be raised in this regard are: What did you learn about your own learning? What sense did you make of the course structure/rationale/assessment plan? How and where can you apply this learning and these skills? What sense do you make of others' interpretations?[7]

Debriefing, online, can take several shapes. It can occur effectively in small-group arrangements, perhaps more effectively in a small group than in a larger group, considering issues of safety and trust. (See group work discussion in Chapter 5.) It can materialize in written documents that are posted online in large or small forums. A debrief could also be submitted in written format to the instructor for his or her formative or summative review. A synchronous debrief could be held if the group is not too large, as synchronicity can begin to lose its shape and effectiveness when there are too many contributors, especially if the exchange is not well facilitated.

Critiques of Self-Assessment

The educators cited above have all attached caveats to the use of self-assessment in academic work. A much more critical assessment was levelled by Dunning, Heath, and Suls (2004) following the results of a psychological study. Investigating self-assessment in the fields of education, health, and the workplace, they concluded:

---

7 Argyris (1990) and Schön (1983) used the "Ladders of Inference" concept to help people make sense of the perceptions, interpretations, and opinions of others. This technique is also used in organizational development to enhance decision making, balance, and community.

Research in education finds that students' assessments of their performance tend to agree only moderately with those of their teachers and mentors. Students seem largely unable to assess how well or poorly they have comprehended material they have just read. They also tend to be over confident in newly learned skills, at times because the common educational practice of massed training appears to promote rapid acquisition of skill—as well as self-confidence—but not necessarily the retention of skill. (p. 69)

As a part of their empirical studies, Dunning, Heath, and Suls (2004) noted that "complete strangers armed only with scant information about an individual can predict that person's skills and abilities almost as well as he or she can, despite the fact that the individual has a lifetime of self-information to draw upon" (p. 71). The authors supported their conclusions with data that provide a critical appraisal of the human condition. Their conclusions have also been posited by other writers on psychological matters such as Snyder (1987), who investigated self-monitoring behaviours in individuals, noting that we regulate and control the ways in which we present ourselves to others in social and interpersonal situations. Snyder's work reflects Goffman's (1959) seminal work on identity; Bandura's (1986, 1971) work on social ambience and the effect of the medium on who we feel we are; and, later, is echoed by Turkle's (1997) and Wenger's (1998) work on technology, community, and identity. Simply put, it's difficult for individuals to know who they are and difficult to present themselves to others, in the style of Lewis Carroll's Alice when she confessed to the Caterpillar that she was not quite herself (Jones, 2005).

Dunning, Heath, and Suls (2004) pointed out that their study was not exhaustive, and they also clarified that, while still considered imperfect, self-assessments could be more reliable in some circumstances than in others. Their suggestions for "good" self-assessment resonate with those documented above: Ensure clear guidelines and criteria and locate the occasions for self-assessment in an appropriate learning environment that supports the underlying purposes and pedagogy of self-assessment. They also noted that "correlations between grades that students gave themselves and teachers' grades were higher in advanced classes than in introductory courses" (p. 85).

Concluding Thoughts

The arguments above highlight several themes: (a) Self-assessment, when conducted appropriately and within a sound context, can assist learners' critical reflection and thinking skills, thus making them more successful and accomplished learners; (b) self-assessment has complex, inherent weaknesses that often spring from our innate humanness; (c) self-assessment should, in most cases, not be used as evaluative tools. That said, online technology and the constructivist paradigm lend themselves well to self-assessment vehicles and can support self-assessment in either group or individual settings.

10 | Summing Up

And now, the end is near
And so I face the final curtain
My friend, I'll say it clear
I'll state my case, of which I'm certain

—Paul Anka, "My Way"

We hope you will forgive us this bit of sentimentality. It's been a long haul through the assessment landscape, and we want to exit well with just a few concluding thoughts.

We feel we have done what we set out to do. We feel our case is certain. As adult educators and online practitioners, we have grown into, researched, experienced, and accepted the concepts and practices that we have outlined here. We live them, and we are delighted to have had the opportunity to write about them.

The book has, throughout these chapters, focused on issues of assessment specifically arising from online learning. We have made clear the caveat that we addressed learning in the social sciences and humanities, which use a certain type of assessment, usually different from hard data or multiple choice–type instruments. We have discussed authentic learning and authentic assessment, learner engagement, and how the affordances of online learning and a constructivist philosophy of teaching and learning provide good opportunities for creating and implementing authentic learning experiences.

We have focused on the grounding of good online practice in the adult education principles of maturity, respect, deep learning, and constructivist pedagogy. From these principles, it is easy to extrapolate the rationale and shape of authentic assessment practices: assessment that aims for practicality, real-life application, and meaningfulness; assessment that offers learners a context for their creativity and productivity; and assessment that provides a good base for sustained learning. Do we believe that those kinds of assessment are already at work in traditional classrooms? No, not really. Do we believe that, in spite of that, they can be introduced into the online experience? Yes, we do! And we have set about explaining how to do that.

In conclusion, then, we summarize with these themes:

- Assessment is an important part of the cycle of learning, which also includes outcomes (what?), strategies (how?), and content. It is an integral part of the planning process and must coalesce with all other aspects of the intended learning experience, whether in terms of course or program.

- Educators must know and understand their own philosophical stance on teaching and learning in order to choose materials, activities, and assessment in a coherent manner.

- Assessment activities and processes will reflect educators' values.

- Authentic assessment presents learners with opportunities to make connections with prior knowledge and to build relationships between their own learning and real-life situations. Authentic assessment is ill-defined and permits learners to engage with open-ended tasks that sustain learning and the learning cycle.

- Online learning provides fertile ground for the creation of authentic assessment and evaluative activities and should be appreciated for its affordances and used to its full capacity.

- Advancing technology opens more doors for authentic assessment and can include social media tools that can be used in conjunction with traditional assessment vehicles, such as essays and reports, but can also be used independently.

- Journals, group work, projects, portfolios, peer-assessment, and self-assessment all provide opportunities for online authentic assessment.

We have been tempted, in the final days of writing and revising, to add more material to this work as more and more good material espousing these themes has appeared, much of it electronically. On social media venues, this material flashes by in an instant, each click opening up a maze—or a rabbit-hole—of sources, inspirations, and ideas. That said, and knowing that a conclusion is not the time to raise new arguments, we cannot help but include this passage from Wiley's (2017) chapter in Jhangiani and Biswas-Diener's newly published book, as it speaks directly to the issue of assessment:

> Substantive intellectual and practical work remains to be done on Open Assessments. First, questions must be answered regarding the integrity and security of assessments that are openly licensed. Second, as students and faculty (neither of whom are trained in creating valid, reliable assessments) create and contribute a wide range of Open Assessments to the community, we will need to develop techniques for evaluating and improving assessments on the ground and contributing these improvements back to the community. (p. 205)

Wiley's chapter, and indeed, the theme of *Open: The Philosophies and Practices That are Revolutionizing Education and Science* (Jhangiani & Biswas-Diener, 2017), confirm that the "age of open," wherever you stand on it, will continue to evoke more disruption to traditional ways and create more excitement and opportunity. To know this is tremendously exciting and academically provocative, but as we lyricized at the beginning of this chapter, our assessment lines have been drawn, our case is clear, and this is, indeed, the final curtain (for now!).

Other Voices
Reflections from the Field

As a part of this project, we asked colleagues from around the world to reflect on assessment in any manner they chose. Their submissions are presented in this appendix. As always, in our humanities and social science academic world, there are varied opinions on what's what, representing a variety of topics that came to mind. This section provides insights on technologies, on strategies, and on philosophies. Knowing our colleagues, we see some of their research interests and personal missions reflected here! And with academic freedom, we recognize that there are many approaches to academic work and assessment. We sincerely thank these colleagues who shared their experience and insights with us.

Wholly Assessing Learning • *Stephen Downes*

I have often been in the position of assessing student work: as a trainer in a computing services company, as a newspaper editor, as a philosophy professor, as a night school teacher introducing people to the Internet, and most recently, as the instructor in multiple MOOCs.

As my experience in assessment grew and became more diverse, I found myself relying less and less on specific metrics and much more on an overall judgment of a person's capacity. Even in technical disciplines like logic and computer science, I found I could easily see whether a person had an overall aptitude for the subject.

When it came to my experience with MOOCs, I was fortunate enough to be able to turn over the task of formal assessment to my colleagues and instead address the whole person, rather than their specific capacity to perform specific tasks. I could see their progress overall through a process of continual engagement—how they responded to me, how they responded to each other, how they interacted with the guests we had in the course.

By the end of the course, I could evaluate individuals through the process of having a short conversation. It's like Sabine Hossenfelder (2016) said: "During a decade of education, we physicists learn more than the tools of the trade; we also learn the walk and talk of the community, shared through countless seminars and conferences, meetings, lectures and papers. After exchanging a few sentences, we can tell if you're one of us. You can't fake our community slang any more than you can fake a local accent in a foreign country." Physicists recognize each other.

When I dispense with the metrics, it's not as if I'm using nothing to assess expertise. I'm using everything to assess expertise. It may look from the outside like an off-the-cuff judgment, but it's the result of a deep understanding of the discipline. When I assess a person, I'm looking at overall fluency, not completion of a certain set of metrics or competencies.

Stephen Downes is a specialist in learning technology, media, and theory for the Information and Communications Technology portfolio at the National Research Council of Canada in Moncton, New Brunswick, Canada.

Assessing Participation • *Ellen Rose*

For me, one of the most challenging aspects of online assessment is the issue of learner participation. When I first began teaching online graduate courses in education, I followed the lead of others, who typically gave a weighted mark for participation. For example, participation in online discussions and learning activities might be worth 20% of a student's overall grade.

However, this commonplace practice soon came to seem problematic. I did not give a participation mark in my classroom-based graduate courses, so why was it necessary in online offerings? If it was intended as an incentive for participation, then surely it was not necessary for adult learners who *wanted* to learn and participate, whether in face-to-face or online courses, and who were able to make intelligent decisions about their learning. Further, it seemed to me that the participation mark was a poor substitute for providing a variety of engaging ways for learners to explore and respond to new content. Finally, I realized that the participation mark benefited those learners who were perhaps less thoughtful but more ready to get online and post their first thoughts, while disadvantaging those who preferred to take the time to reflect more deeply before going public with their perspectives. The result was often an overwhelming quantity of banal discussion posts offered as evidence of "participation."

However, when I tried removing the participation mark in an online course, there was an immediate outcry from my students. They wanted their participation assessed, in recognition of the fact that participation in online course is often challenging and time-consuming. A group activity that might take 20 minutes for five students sitting around a table can take an entire week for five students working together asynchronously.

My current approach, a kind of negotiation between these two competing perspectives, involves asking learners to assess their own participation. At the beginning of the course, we agree on a set of indicators, which becomes a rubric they can use to think critically about their own involvement and contributions. Importantly, the indicators emphasize quality rather than quantity.

Ellen Rose teaches in the Faculty of Education's doctoral program at the University of New Brunswick, in Fredericton, New Brunswick, Canada.

Voice Marking • *Terry Anderson*

In the online graduate program that I teach in, most of the assessment consists of student essays, reports or examination of artifacts such as business plans, e-portfolios, or learning design documentation. I'm not a fast typist, so I find the work of doing a thorough assessment and recommendations for improvement to be time consuming. Thus, I was intrigued when I heard Phil Ice present data on voice marking at a conference.

The technique I have settled on involves saving students' work as PDF files and then using the annotation tools that are built into Adobe Acrobat to insert voice snippets. These then appear throughout the text as clickable speaker icons that the student listens to as they review my feedback and assessment. The feedback from students has been almost 100% positive. I know I can be much more relaxed using voice and let my "teaching presence" shine! I can also be more informal. But most importantly, this technique saves me time, and the amount of feedback provided is greatly expanded compared to what I used to provide by typing.

One lesson was learnt, though, when I inserted a comment—"Praise the Lord, after two pages we finally come to the topic of the essay!" The student accused me of blasphemy!

I did have some technical issues. For some reason, on a Mac, one can't throttle back the recording speed of the internal microphone, so I purchased an external mic. The high fidelity doesn't really make a difference to the voice quality, but the resulting size of the PDF file can become huge, especially in longer documents such as complete theses. One can also use built-in tools for Word, but at least in past versions, the resulting file size prevented returning via email.

The research literature supports both the time saving and the almost universal enthusiasm from students when using this type of feedback. I am sure that there are now tools that allow video as well as voice, but once again file size may become problematic with more media in play. In any case, the students probably get quite enough of my "presence" (and bad haircut!) with just the voice.

Terry Anderson, Professor Emeritus, Athabasca University, and editor of the Issues in Distance Education series from Athabasca University Press.

Authentic Assessment Using Audio • *Archie Zariski*

The field of alternative dispute resolution has expanded significantly in the 21st century as courts, agencies, and corporations have embraced the practices of arbitration, conciliation, and mediation. Athabasca University's course of the same name is intended to introduce students to the theory and practice of conflict and dispute resolution. Because media-tion is widespread, the course attempts to give students some first-hand experience of what it is like to act as a mediator.

Mediators use a toolbox of skills and techniques to help disputing par-ties see common interests and pathways to agreement. Active listening and providing constructive feedback are two key capacities mediators must develop. In order to assess learning of such skills online, we adopted two oral assignments that reflected common practices of mediators: First, students submitted their presentation of a mediator's opening statement to the parties in conflict to introduce them to the process; and second, students submitted their response as mediators to hearing one party's statement of their grievance.

The free recording program Audacity is recommended to students for completing these assignments, but they may submit an audio file using whatever program they have. For the second assignment, I recorded a monologue of a disputant that is played for students and that they must then carefully summarize back as they would in a mediation conference. I believe these assignments represent authentic assessments that help students learn about the complex task of acting as a mediator.

Student reactions to the course have included: "I really enjoy the audio assignments"; "I liked the oral assignments. They required me to learn to do them, but also pushed me there, and to record the role of a mediator was very applicable to the learning objectives of this course"; and, "this course was relevant and well-structured to teach students, not just test their memorization."

Archie Zariski, LLM, teaches legal studies at Athabasca University.

Negotiated Assessment • *Beth Perry*

I have come to the conclusion that the adult learners I teach in online courses value thorough and thoughtful feedback from the instructor, and, importantly, they also value evaluation. That is, they are motivated by reaching for (and achieving) a grade that they view as success. My teaching philosophy is founded on William Purkey's (1992) invitational theory, which focuses on trust, respect, optimism, and intentionality. My approaches to student assessment and evaluation are structured to take these four pillars into consideration.

One graduate course I teach has content related to becoming an effective educator of health professionals. This course is structured to provide learners the opportunity (within parameters) to create their own course assignments and evaluation guidelines for those assignments. That is, students are required to produce one descriptive artifact and two analytic artifacts as evidence of achieving the course learning outcomes. The format of these artifacts can include written, video, or audio aspects, and the details of each artifact (including how it will be assessed) is negotiated with the instructor during the first weeks of the course.

The course incorporates invitational principles of respect, as learners have choice in how they will demonstrate their learning. Having choice respects individual differences and helps to personalize learning. Trust is enhanced as learners come to know that their viewpoint, preferences, and learning goals matter to the course instructor. The learning they have chosen matters to them and their personal and professional goals.

As the instructor, I have a one-to-one relationship with each learner as their plans for the assignment are determined in a contractual manner at the outset of the course. Assessment becomes an integrated and very intentional element of each artifact. Everything students do in this course becomes meaningful to them and their assignments, and the instructor's contribution in terms of responses and feedback to those assignments is personalized.

The lesson learned from teaching this course is that students are often uncomfortable at first with the apparent openness of this assessment design. They want to know what they have to do to get a certain grade. Learners seem more familiar with assessment strategies where requirements are clearly stated by the instructor in the course syllabus. Instructional time spent one-to-one with learners helping them to embrace this approach is considerable. However, the benefits to the learners seem worth this investment.

As a side note, I find teaching a class with a more invitational and personalized assessment plan challenging, intellectually stimulating, and less monotonous than marking multiple papers on the same topic. As an added benefit I become well acquainted with each learner early in the course, and this relationship enhances our experience over the duration of the learning.

Beth Perry teaches online graduate and undergraduate courses in the Faculty of Health Disciplines at Athabasca University.

The Value of Feedback and Revision • *Julie Shattuck*

My approach to assessment is directly linked to my own experiences as an online student. What I appreciated the most from my professors was timely, detailed feedback that helped me move forward as a learner. It strikes me as ironic that, as a doctoral candidate, I received more help on how to improve as a writer than I had at any other time in my academic journey. My professors treated me as an apprentice writer and afforded me multiple opportunities to revise my work before it was assessed.

I pay my positive assessment experiences forward to my online students who are in their undergraduate English composition courses. I encourage collaborative assessment by first exposing students to the benefits of participating in a structured peer-review process. I give examples of feedback I've received on my writing, which shows students that there is no such thing as a perfect writer and also models what kind of feedback is most useful in helping a writer produce their best work. We discuss how hard it is to share writing, especially in the online environment, but by building a strong community of learners, I help students build trust in each other. After students revise their peer-reviewed essays, they submit their work to me. I give students prompt feedback on a few major areas that would help them improve their writing without overwhelming them with every detail that could be revised. I encourage students to reflect on this feedback and use my comments and their reactions to the comments to revise their essays for regrading. Not all students take me up on this opportunity, and that's fine, as not all students want to raise their initial grade. For me, giving students the opportunity to judge for themselves whether the grade they earn initially ends up being their final grade is an important step in helping students become able and confident writers.

Julie Shattuck teaches English courses both online and on-campus at Frederick Community College.

Guided Interactive Self-Assessment • *Dianne Conrad*

The master's course that I teach at Athabasca University is housed in the Centre for Distance Education although it is a course on adult and lifelong learning. As we have pointed out in this book, these two areas of education are very closely related and so the placement of this course within the Centre for Distance Education makes sense. What is continually surprising to me is that the study of adult learning is quite new to many if not most of my students, who come to it from a variety of program areas.

The learning journeys of these "new-to-adult-education" learners were often steep climbs, and it became important to me to engage them in self-reflection along the way. Any graduate student should be able to crank out a research paper with good criteria and instructions. But what were they experiencing and what did they themselves think about their own learning and engagement in this course? I introduced a learning journal in which they were invited to reflect on their learning, related to course discussions, materials, and interactions, all along the way. I emphasized that the journal's focus was "you," rather than an external topic. These documents turned out to be extremely long, intense, and revealing reads. Unfortunately, given the nature of the assignment, they were due at the end of the course, and I didn't have the chance to learn from their experiences in time to do anything or reply meaningfully.

I therefore moved the submission date forward a couple of weeks. Taking two weeks away from their writing time did not shorten the length of the journals! But it gave me time to fully digest their reflections and respond to them using Track Changes on the file. (I will work on changing those responses to voice.) Finally, adopting Schön's (1983) reflection-on-action notion, I ask learners to self-assess their course experience in three categories: reflections on a certain very powerful group experience; last-minute insight on their learning experience during the course; and five adjectives that describe them as learners. This short document (a two-pager) is due right at the end of the course and provides learners with another opportunity for self-reflection on their performance. It summarizes, affirms, and complements journal themes, while also giving me another chance to provide feedback or comment on what I have observed or read.

The response to this assignment, which constitutes a lot of writing by students, has been overwhelmingly positive. The work is generally of very high quality. As instructor, I hear what is *really* going on with them as learners, the highs and lows, and I can plainly see their struggles as they try to make sense of concepts and theories. These documents take a long time to read, but my own learning from them is time so well spent.

Implications of an Experiment Measuring Teacher Satisfaction against Performance • *Rory McGreal*

Many years ago, in an unnamed university, more than 100 teachers taught the same English as a Second Language program to more than 1,000 pre-university students. All teachers were constrained to teach the same content in a similar way. All students took exactly the same examination on completion of the full-year program. They also completed teacher evaluations.

As a research project, the teacher evaluations were divided into three groups: positive, negative, and other (those either not understood or neutral). The prediction was that those students with teachers who received a positive evaluation would do significantly better than those who were in classes with teachers who received a negative evaluation. Even a cursory analysis showed that there was no discernible difference between the two groups. A statistical analysis also showed no significant difference between the results of teachers with positive student evaluations and those with negative student evaluations.

This experience relates to one's position regarding the need for an objective assessment. It is very easy for either students or teachers to mistakenly assume that learning has occurred. If students feel good about a teacher or the course, then they may judge that they have mastered the content or skills being taught. Because the students feel good and are positive in the class, the teacher too may assume that the concepts and/or skills have been mastered. That is why, in my opinion, objective tests of achievement are an important if not essential part of the learning process, at least in formal situations. Of course, learners can acquire knowledge and skills on their own, but at some point this needs to be tested for confirmation. Tests may be informal or formal.

Rory McGreal is the UNESCO/Commonwealth of Learning/International Council for Open and Distance Education Chairholder in Open Educational Resources and professor at Athabasca University.

E-Portfolios and Journals as Reflective Tools for Assessment • *Lisa Marie Blaschke*

In recent years, I've moved away from typical assessment measures, such as the written essay or summative quiz. Instead, I have started evaluating students along a continuum, applying formative assessment, which allows me to give feedback that supports students' ongoing learning and development and their ability to improve on their work as they progress along the learning path. Some of the key learning tools within this context are the online e-portfolio and the reflective journal (or blog) that students keep as part of their e-portfolio, which showcases their acquired skills and competencies. With each set of learning-journal reflections that students post, I give them feedback on areas for further exploration and research, and ways in which they can improve upon their learning approach. The learning journal not only gives students an opportunity to reflect on what they have learned and how they have learned it but also gives me a window into the student experience, insight into their abilities, and an idea of what interests them most. Their learning journals give me insight into what concepts or ideas they are struggling with, what motivates them, what inspires them (and what doesn't), how they learn best, and where they need support. I like this kind of assessment because it gives students an opportunity to improve on what they have done and an ongoing investment in their work, and allows me to coach them as they progress along the learning path.

Lisa Marie Blaschke is associate professor (adjunct) at the University of Maryland University College and program director of the Master of Distance Education and E-Learning program at Carl von Ossietzky University of Oldenburg.

Assessment in Online Learning Using Social Networks • *Gürhan Durak*

For about three years, I have been teaching my undergraduate and postgraduate courses either fully online or as hybrids. The name of the course that I have taught fully online is "Scientific Ethics." We teach all our courses via Edmodo, a leader among social-learning networks, where learners can share any kind of resources, announcements, and files. Another advantage of this system is that it provides mobile support. When learners install the mobile application on their smart phones, they can instantly see the course-related sharing. In this way, they are simultaneously informed about any sharing done via the system, about any resource uploaded on the system, and about any homework assigned via the system. In this case, the user does not have to log into the system to see the resources uploaded on the system in online asynchronous applications. Learners also participate in live lessons as part of the course.

Within the scope of the course, on a weekly basis, I share resources related to the videos. Learners, after studying with the help of these resources, respond to the questions directed to them in front of the video camera. These applications, repeated on a weekly basis, are evaluated and given to the learners as feedback (in the form of homework scores and comments) until the following week. The course is executed in this way until midterm and end-of-year exams, which are administered using the exam application on Edmodo.

In these exams, we use various question types such as open-ended, multiple choice, fill in the blank, and matching. During the exam, learners record themselves using a webcam (from a certain angle and at a certain distance). In this way, we can confirm that there is nobody else near the learner during the exam and that they are focused on just the exam. (In the past, when I once gave an exam for an online course, I had doubts about whether the learners took the exam alone or with a companion. Therefore, for the last two years, I ask them to video-record the exam process). At the end of the exam, learners upload the video-record and the exam file on the system and complete the process.

At the end of academic terms, I hold individual interviews with learners who give positive feedback on the course format and strategies used in the teaching of the course. I feel that this method is useful for evaluation, which is one of the most problematic aspects of distance education, and I recommend it.

Gürhan Durak teaches undergraduate and master's-level courses in the department of Computer Education and Instructional Technologies at Balıkesir University in Turkey.

Using Quizzes for Assessment in a Negotiation Massive Open Online Course • *Noam Ebner*

In negotiation courses, assessment is one area in which there is a great deal of variation between teachers. Teachers strive to apply multiple methods of assessment, many of which require a great deal of effort and time investment per student.

As I prepared to teach a MOOC on Negotiation, I realized that the scale of a MOOC requires a different approach to assessment. I was concerned about the validity of the two models MOOCs have converged around—automated multiple-choice quizzes graded by the system, and peer-assessment systems—for providing summative assessment. Quizzes test only for certain types of learning; succeeding can be more a matter of quiz skills than of content understanding. Peer-review relegates assessment to non-experts. Both systems have offered up new opportunities for plagiarism and cheating.

Upon reflection, I realized that my search for valid methods for summative feedback was based more on habit than on any real need. The not-for-credit nature of the MOOC actually eliminated the necessity of providing summative assessment. Only those students completing the course and requesting a certificate of completion (on average, about 5% of students who register for a MOOC) required any form of summative assessment to determine whether their work achieved a minimal performance bar. For the large majority of my students, I could focus on providing formative assessment. One element of this manifested itself in offering formative feedback somewhat camouflaged as an ordinarily summative assessment method, the multiple-choice quiz.

Each of the course's four weekly modules included a five-question multiple-choice quiz. At the end of the course there was an additional 15-question quiz. These quizzes had different purposes. The weekly quizzes provided only formative assessment; once a completed quiz was submitted, the system would indicate which questions were answered correctly. It would also provide the correct answer to questions answered incorrectly and direct the student to the specific piece of course content in which the answer could be found. Participants could take these quizzes as many times as desired, until they were sure they had understood all the material by aceing it. However, the grade achieved on this quiz was *not* recorded by the system; it only recorded the fact that a particular student had *taken* the quiz. *Taking* the quizzes, not "passing" them, was a requirement for those students wishing to receive a certificate of completion. Another formative purpose of the weekly quizzes was familiarizing students with the quiz platform and typical questions—preparing them for taking the course's final quiz.

The final quiz provided a combination of formative and summative assessment. In addition to providing the formative input described above, this quiz was also graded. A student scoring 10/15 correct answers fulfilled this certification requirement. A student dissatisfied with the quiz score could take it one additional time, with a partially new set of questions generated from the question bank. Once again, there was a formative purpose underlying this summative structure: Students were incentivized to review the correct and incorrect answers on their first attempt, as they would thereby improve their odds for succeeding the second time around.

Noam Ebner is professor of Negotiation and Conflict Resolution in the Department of Interdisciplinary Studies at Creighton University.

Integrating Assessment into the Learning Cycle • *Susan Bainbridge*

Completing a written assignment is often assumed to be the equivalent of taking a test: By writing a paper, a student is expected to demonstrate particular abilities and knowledge. But I want my students to *learn* from the activity as well. When students are asked to submit papers, I assess their work on the basis of criteria that have been shared with the students in advance and then return their papers to them. At that point, I do not want my students simply to look at their grade, perhaps quickly scan my comments, and then move on. I want them to *learn* how to create a better submission. With this goal in mind, I ask them to revise their papers and resubmit them. Then I grade the second submission as the final one. Now the paper has become a teaching tool, and, by making changes, students hopefully will have incorporated new knowledge. Students are expected to read my initial comments and then make use of them. The grades are naturally higher with their final submissions, but so is the quality of their work. Assessment should be part of the learning process. Otherwise, it is of no significant value, as students will simply continue to make the same errors.

Although I currently teach at the graduate level, I have used this approach in undergraduate instruction as well, and it works extremely well in online courses. I can track changes to papers and add voice comments, and, if need be, the student and I can Skype once the first draft is returned. The process not only enables students to learn from their mistakes but also helps to build a healthy rapport between the instructor and the learner.

Susan Bainbridge earned a Doctor of Education in Distance Education from Athabasca University, where she currently holds an adjunct appointment.

In Praise of Authentic Assessment • *Jon Dron*

With rare exceptions (where intense, lonely pressure is authentic to the task, such as in some kinds of journalism), I hate invigilated, written examinations: They are normally unfair, inauthentic, weakly discriminatory, hugely stressful and, above all, make a negative contribution to the learning process by making motivation entirely extrinsic and teacher-controlled. They are not even cheap: it's not cost-effective to incorporate something into the teaching process that actively militates against learning. And they don't even do the one job they are supposed to do well at all. In some countries, four out of five students admit to exam cheating, and more than half admit to it in most countries, including Canada. That's an inevitable consequence of making them the point of learning, and it is entirely our own fault.

I have steadfastly avoided exams in my own courses, using combinations of techniques like personally chosen projects, embedding the sharing of work with other students, negotiable personal outcomes, portfolios of flexible evidence, shared reflective diaries, community building, giving feedback on achievement but never grades on assignments, and so on. Every activity contributes to both individual learning and to the learning of others, gives learners control, and is personally relevant and uniquely challenging for every learner. Feedback is only ever supportive, never judgmental, and inherent in the process. In combination, this makes cheating highly improbable, but it always involves me in yet another fight with those that believe exams are the gold standard of reliable summative testing and that nothing else will do. One of my colleagues, persuaded by my arguments but not willing to face the wrath of colleagues by removing exams, has found a nice halfway solution. After following an open, social, reflective, project-oriented process throughout his courses, he simply requires students on the final exam to write about what they did, with a structured reflective framework to help guide them. They know this in advance, so there's relatively little pressure. It is only possible for those who actually did the work to do this, and, more importantly, it serves a very useful pedagogical purpose that helps to consolidate, connect, and reinforce what they have learned. The main complaint students have about it is that they get writer's cramp because they write so much.

Jon Dron is a member of the Technology Enhanced Knowledge Research Institute and chair of the School of Computing and Information Systems at Athabasca University, as well as an Honorary Faculty Fellow in the Centre for Learning and Teaching at the University of Brighton.

References

Akyol, Z., & Garrison, D. R. (2008). The development of a community of inquiry over time in an online course: Understanding the progression and integration of social, cognitive and teaching presence. *Journal of Asynchronous Learning Networks, 12*(3), 3–22.

Akyol, Z., Garrison, D. R., & Ozden, M. (2009). Online and blended communities of inquiry: Exploring the developmental and perceptional differences. *International Review of Research in Open and Distributed Learning, 10*(6). Retrieved from http://www.irrodl.org/index.php/irrodl/article/view/765

Albrecht, B. (2006). *Enriching student experience through blended learning.* Boulder, CO: Education Center for Applied Research. Retrieved from http://www.ammanu.edu.jo/EN/Content/HEC/2.pdf

Allen, C. (2004). Tracing the Evolution of Social Software [Blog post]. Retrieved from http://www.lifewithalacrity.com/2004/10/tracing_the_evo.html

Allen, I. E., & Seaman, J. (2015). *Grade level: Tracking online education in the United States.* Babson Survey Research Group and Quahog Research Group, LLC. Retrieved from https://www.onlinelearningsurvey.com/reports/gradelevel.pdf

Allen, I. E., & Seaman, J. (2016). *Online report card: Tracking online education in the United States.* Babson Survey Research Group and Quahog Research Group, LLC. Retrieved from https://onlinelearningsurvey.com/reports/onlinereportcard.pdf

Anderson, C. (2006). Wisdom of the crowds: Scientific publishers should let their online readers become reviewers. *Nature.* doi:10.1038/nature04992

Anderson, T. (2003). Getting the mix right: An update and theoretical rationale for interaction. *International Review of Research in Open and Distributed Learning, 4*(2). Retrieved from http://www.irrodl.org/index.php/irrodl/article/view/149

Anderson, T. (2004). Towards a theory of online learning. In T. Anderson & F. Elloumi (Eds.), *The theory and practice of online learning* (pp. 33–60). Edmonton, AB: Athabasca University.

Anderson, T. (2008). Teaching in an online learning context. In T. Anderson (Ed.), *The theory and practice of online learning* (2nd ed., pp. 343–365). Edmonton, AB: Athabasca University Press. Retrieved from http://www.aupress.ca/books/120146/ebook/02_Anderson_2008-Theory_and_Practice_of_Online_Learning.pdf

Anderson, T. (2008). Towards a theory of online learning. In T. Anderson (Ed.), *The theory and practice of online learning.* (2nd ed., pp. 45–74). Edmonton, AB: Athabasca University Press. Retrieved from http://www.aupress.ca/books/120146/ebook/02_Anderson_2008-Theory_and_Practice_of_Online_Learning.pdf

Anderson, T., & Garrison, D. R. (1998). Learning in a networked world: New roles and responsibilities. In C. Gibson (Ed.), *Distance learners in higher education: Institutional responses for quality outcomes* (pp. 97–112). Madison, WI: Atwood Publishing.

Angelo, T, & Cross, K. P. (1993). *Classroom assessment techniques: A handbook for college teachers.* San Francisco, CA: Jossey-Bass.

Argyris, C. (1990). *Overcoming organizational defences: Facilitating organizational learning.* Needham, MA: Allyn and Bacon.

Ascough, R. S. (2011). Learning (about) outcomes: How the focus on assessment can help overall course design. *Canadian Journal of Higher Education, 41*(2), 44–61.

Astin, A.W., Banta, T. W., Cross, K. P., El-Khawas, E., Ewell, P. T., Hutchings, P., . . . Wright, B. D. (1992, December). Principles of good practice for assessing student learning. *American Association for Higher Education Assessment Forum.* Retrieved from http://www.learningoutcomesassessment.org/PrinciplesofAssessment.html

Ausubel, D. (1978). In defense of advance organizers: A reply to the critics. *Review of Educational Research, 48*(20), 251–257.

Bandura, A. (1971). *Social learning theory.* Morristown, NJ: General Learning Press.

Bandura, A. (1986). *Social foundations of thought and action: A social cognitive theory.* Englewood Cliffs, NJ: Prentice-Hall.

Barber, W., King, S., & Buchanan, S. (2015). Problem based learning and authentic assessment in digital pedagogy: Embracing the role of collaborative communities. *Electronic Journal of E-Learning, 13*(2), 59–67.

Barnard, J. (2016). Tweets as microfiction: On Twitter's live nature and 140-character limit as tools for developing storytelling skills. *New Writing: The*

International Journal for the Practice & Theory of Creative Writing, 13(1), 3–16. doi:10.1080/14790726.2015.1127975

Barnett, R., & Coate, K. (2005). *Engaging the curriculum in higher education.* New York, NY: Open University Press.

Barr, R. B., & Tagg, J. (1995). From teaching to learning: A new paradigm for undergraduate education. *Change, 27*(6), 12–26.

Barrett, H. (2000). *Electronic portfolios = multimedia development + portfolio development: The electronic development process.* Retrieved from http://electronicportfolios.org/portfolios/EPDevProcess.html

Bates, A. W. (2008). Transforming distance education through new technologies. In T. Evans, M. Haughey, & D. Murphy (Eds.), *International Handbook of Distance Education* (pp. 217–236). Bingley, UK: Emerald Group.

Benson, A. D. (2002). Using online learning to meet workforce demand. *Quarterly Review of Distance Education, 3*(4), 443–452.

Bereiter, C., & Scardamalia, M. (1987). *The psychology of written composition.* Hillsdale, NJ: Erlbaum.

Biemiller, L. (2014, June 9). Latest Christensen disruption: Crowdsourced journal article. *Chronicle of Higher Education.* Retrieved from https://www.chronicle.com/blogs/wiredcampus/latest-christensen-disruption-crowdsourced-journal-article/53153

Bishop, J. L., & Verlager, M.A. (2013). *The flipped classroom: A survey of the research.* 120th ASEE Annual Conference & Exposition. Retrieved from https://www.asee.org/public/conferences/20/papers/6219/view

Biswas-Diener, R., & Jhangiani, R. S. (2017). Introduction to Open. In R. S. Jhangiani & R. Biswas-Diener (Eds.). *Open: The Philosophy and Practices that are Revolutionizing Education and Science* (pp. 3–7). London, UK: Ubiquity Press. doi:10.5334/bbc.a

Black, P., & Wiliam, D. (1998). Assessment and classroom learning. *Education: Principles, Policy and Practice, 5*(1), 7–74.

Blanton, W. E., Moorman, G., & Trathen, W. (1998). Telecommunications and teacher education: A social constructivist review. *Review of Research in Education, 23,* 235–275.

Bloom, B. S. (1956). *Taxonomy of Educational Objectives, Handbook I: The Cognitive Domain.* New York, NY: David McKay Co.

Bloom, B. S. (1969). Some theoretical issues relating to educational evaluation. In R. W. Tyler (Ed.), *Educational evaluation: New roles, new means. National Society for the Study of Education Yearbook, 68*(2), 26–50. Chicago, IL: University of Chicago Press.

Bloxham, S. (2009) Marking and moderation in the UK: False assumptions and wasted resources. *Assessment & Evaluation in Higher Education, 34*(2), 209–220.

Boitshwarelo, B. (2011). Proposing an integrated research framework for connectivism: Utilising theoretical synergies. *International Review of Research in Open and Distribution Learning, 12*(3). Retrieved from http://www.irrodl. org/index.php/irrodl/article/view/881

Bok, D. (2006). *Our underachieving colleges: A candid look at how much students learn and why they should be learning more.* Princeton, NJ: Princeton University Press.

Bountrogianni, M. (2015, July 8). Six ways continuing education can close Canada's skills gap. *Huffington Post.* Retrieved from http://www. huffingtonpost.ca/dr-marie-bountrogianni/adult-education-second-career_b_7737592.html

Bowness, S. (2014, January 15). Tracking the learning journey through e-portfolios. *University Affairs.* Retrieved from www.universityaffairs.ca/.../ tracking-the-learning-journey-through-e-por

Brame, C. (2013). Flipping the classroom. Vanderbilt University Center for Teaching. Retrieved from http://cft.vanderbilt.edu/guides-sub-pages/flipping-the-classroom

Brookfield, S. D. (1990a). *The skillful teacher: On technique, trust, and responsiveness in the classroom.* San Francisco, CA: Jossey-Bass.

Brookfield, S. D. (1990b). *Understanding and facilitating adult learning: A comprehensive analysis of principles and effective practices.* San Francisco, CA: Jossey-Bass.

Brown, J. S, & Adler, R. P. (2008). Minds on fire: Open education, the long tail, and learning 2.0. *EDUCAUSE Review, 43*(1), 16–32. Retrieved from https:// er.educause.edu/articles/2008/1/minds-on-fire-open-education-the-long-tail-and-learning-20

Bull, B. (2015). Learning beyond letter grades: Exploring the promise, power & possibility of feedback & assessment [Webinar] In *EDUCAUSE.* Retrieved from https://events.educause.edu/eli/courses/2015/eli-course-learning-beyond-letter-grades-exploring-the-promise--possibility-of-assessment

Bullen, M. (1998). Participation and critical thinking in online university distance education. *Journal of Distance Education, 13*(2), 1–32.

Burge, E., Gibson, C., & Gibson, T. (2011). *Flexible pedagogy, flexible practice: Notes from the trenches of distance education.* Edmonton, AB: Athabasca University Press.

Butler, C. J. (2004, December). *Equal and fair are not the same: Classroom issues of fairness.* T-TAC Network News, Old Dominion University. Retrieved from www.ttac.odu.edu/newsletter/PDF/OLD/Nov_Dec_2004_Jan_2005/Page2. pdf

Caldwell, J. E. (2007). Clickers in the large classroom: Current research and best-practice tips. *Life Sciences Education, 6*(1), 9–20.

Campbell, K., & Schwier, R. A. (2014). Major movements in instructional design. In O. Zawacki-Richter & T. Anderson (Eds.), *Online distance education: Towards a research agenda* (pp. 345–380). Edmonton, AB: Athabasca University Press.

Canadian Association for Adult Education. (1943). *Manifesto of the CAAE.* Toronto, ON: CAAE.

Candy, P. C. (1991). *Self-direction for lifelong learning: A comprehensive guide to theory and practice.* San Francisco, CA: Jossey-Bass.

Carnevale, A. P. (2016). Higher education and democratic capitalism. *Educause Review, 51*(6), 10–26. Retrieved from https://er.educause.edu/articles/2016/10/higher-education-and-democratic-capitalism

Casilli, C., & Hickey, D. (2016). Transcending conventional credentialing and assessment paradigms with information-rich digital badges. *Information Society, 32*(2), 117–129. doi:10.1080/01972243.2016.1130500

Center for Innovative Teaching and Learning. . (2015). *Teaching handbook.* University of Indiana. Retrieved from https://citl.indiana.edu/files/pdf/teaching_handbook.pdf

Cheng, X., Nolan, T., & Macaulay, L. (2013). Don't give up the community: A viewpoint of trust development in online collaboration. *Information Technology & People, 26*(3), 298–318.

Christensen, C.M. (1997). *The innovator's dilemma: When new technologies cause great firms to fail.* Boston, MA: Harvard Business School Press.

Christensen, G., Steinmetz, A., Alcorn, B., Bennett, A. Woods, D. & Emanuel, E. J. (2013). *The MOOC phenomenon: Who takes massive open online courses and why?* SSRN working paper. Retrieved from https://papers.ssrn.com/sol3/papers.cfm?abstract_id=2350964

Ciampa, K., & Gallagher, T. (2015). Blogging to enhance in-service teachers' professional learning and development during collaborative inquiry. *Educational Technology Research and Development, 63*(6), 883–913. doi:10.1007/s11423-015-9404-7

Cleveland-Innes, M., Shea, P., & Swan, K. (2007, November). Back to the future: What's next for the online community of inquiry? Presentation to *The Sloan-C 13th Annual Asynchronous Learning Networks Conference.* Orlando, Florida.

Collaboration for Online Higher Education and Research (COHERE). (2016). *Report on blended learning.* Ottawa, ON: HRSDC. Retrieved from http://cohere.

ca/wp-content/uploads/2017/09/REPORT-ON-BLENDED-LEARNING-FINAL1.pdf

Colby, A., Ehrlich, T., Beaumont, E., & Stephens, J. (2003). *Educating citizens: Preparing America's undergraduates for lives of moral and civic responsibility.* San Francisco, CA: Jossey-Bass.

Community of Inquiry (CoI) website. (n.d.). Retrieved from https://coi.athabascau.ca/

Conrad, D. (2002). Deep in the hearts of learners: Insights into the nature of online community. *Journal of Distance Education, 17*(1), 1–19.

Conrad, D. (2004). University instructors' reflections on their first online teaching experiences. *Journal of Asynchronous Learning Networks, 8*(2), 31–44.

Conrad, D. (2005). Building and maintaining community in cohort-based online learning. *Journal of Distance Education, 20*(1), 1–21.

Conrad, D. (2006). The plain hard work of teaching online: Strategies for instructors. In M. Bullen & D. James (Eds.), *Making the transition to e-learning: Strategies and issues* (pp. 191–207). Hersey, PA: Information Science Publishing.

Conrad, D. (2009). Cognitive, instructional, and social presence as factors in learners' negotiation of planned absences from online study. *International Review of Research in Open and Distributed Learning, 10*(3). Retrieved from http://www.irrodl.org/index.php/irrodl/article/viewArticle/630/1261

Conrad, D. (2011). The role of language in portfolio learning. *International Review of Research in Open and Distributed Learning, 12*(1), 109–123. Retrieved from http://www.irrodl.org/index.php/irrodl/article/view/1062

Conrad, D. (2013). Assessment challenges in open learning: Way-finding, fork in the road, or end of the line? *Open Praxis, 5*(1), 41–47. Retrieved from http://openpraxis.org/index.php/OpenPraxis/issue/current/showToc

Conrad, D. (2014). Interaction and communication in online learning communities: Toward an engaged and flexible future. In O. Zawacki-Richter & T. Anderson (Eds.), *Online distance education: Towards a research agenda* (pp. 381–402). Edmonton, AB: Athabasca University Press.

Conrad, D., & Wardrop, E. (2010). Exploring the relationship of mentoring to knowledge-building in RPL practice. *Canadian Journal for Studies in Adult Education, 23*(1), 1–22.

Contact North. (2012). Online learning as a critical component of long term institutional strategy: Perspectives among Ontario college and university presidents. Retrieved from http://teachonline.ca/sites/default/files/perspectives_from_college_and_university_presidents1.pdf

Contact North. (2016). Top 10 Wish List for Online Learning in 2016. Retrieved from http://teachonline.ca/tools-trends/top-10-wish-list-for-online-learning-in-2016

Council of Ontario Universities. (2011). Ensuring the value of university degrees in Ontario. Retrieved from http://cou.on.ca/reports/ensuring-the-value-of-university-degrees/

Cranton, P. (1998). Transformative learning: Individual growth and development through critical reflection. In S. M. Scott, B. Spencer, & A. M. Thomas (Eds.), *Learning for life: Canadian readings in adult education* (pp. 188–199). Toronto, ON: Thompson Educational Publishing.

Cranton, P. (2013). Adult learning theory. In T. Nesbit, S. Brigham, & N. Taber (Eds.), *Building on critical traditions: Adult education and learning in Canada* (pp. 95–106). Toronto: Thompson Educational Publishing.

Cranton, P., & Carusetta, E. (2004). Perspectives on authenticity in teaching. *Adult Education Quarterly, 55*(1), 5–22.

Cronenweth, S. (2012). Peer assessment in MOOCs and online courses [Blog post]. Retrieved from http://blog.socrato.com/peer-assessment-in-moocs-and-online-courses/

Cross, K. P. (1981). *Adults as learners.* San Francisco, CA: Jossey-Bass.

Daniel, J. (2012). Making sense of MOOCs: Musings in a maze of myth, paradox and possibility [Research paper]. Seoul: Korean National Open University. Retrieved from https://www.tonybates.ca/wp-content/uploads/Making-Sense-of-MOOCs.pdf

Daniel, J. (2016). Combatting corruption and enhancing integrity: A contemporary challenge for the quality and credibility of higher education. Advisory Statement for Effective International Practice. Washington, DC: CHEA/CIQG IIEP-UNESCO.

Darkenwald, G., & Merriam, S. (1982). *Adult education: Foundations of practice.* New York, NY: Harper & Row.

Davidson, C. (2014, March 14). Changing higher education to change the world [Blog post]. Retrieved from http://chronicle.com/blogs/future/2014/03/14/changing-higher-education-to-change-the-world/

DeCoursey, T. (2006). The pros and cons of open peer review: Should authors be told who their reviewers are? *Nature.* doi: 10.1038/nature04991

Deller, F., Brumwell, S., & MacFarlane, A. (2015). *The language of learning outcomes: Definitions and assessments.* Toronto, ON: Higher Education Quality Council of Ontario.

Dewey, J. (1933). *How we think: A restatement of the relation of reflective thinking to the educative process* (Rev. ed.). Boston, MA: D. C. Heath.

Dewey, J. (1938). *Experience and education.* New York, NY: Macmillan.

Diamond, R. M. (2008). *Designing and assessing courses and curricula: A practical guide.* San Francisco, CA: Jossey-Bass.

Downes, S. (2010, December). Fairness and equity in education [Blog post]. Retrieved from https://www.huffingtonpost.com/stephen-downes/democratizing-education_b_794925.html

Downes, S. (2011, September). Why #connectivism is not a learning theory [Blog post]. Retrieved from https://www.downes.ca/post/56199

Draper, J. (1991). Understanding values in workplace education. In M. C. Taylor, G. R. Lewe, & J. A. Draper (Eds.). *Basic skills for the workplace* (pp. 85–106). Toronto, ON: Culture Concepts.

Dreon, O. (2014, July 23). Formative assessment: The secret sauce of blended success. Retrieved from https://www.facultyfocus.com/articles/blended-flipped-learning/formative-assessment-secret-sauce-blended-success/

Dron, J. (2007). *Control and constraint in e-learning: Choosing when to choose.* Hershey, PA: Idea Group.

Dron, J. (2014). Innovation and change: Changing how we change. In O. Zawacki-Richter & T. Anderson (Eds.), *Online distance education: Towards a research agenda* (pp. 237–265). Edmonton, AB: Athabasca University Press.

Duncan, A. (2011, September 15). Digital badges for learning [Remarks by Secretary Duncan at the 4th Annual Launch of the MacArthur Foundation Digital Media and Lifelong Learning Competition]. Retrieved from http://www.ed.gov/news/speeches/digital-badges-learning

Dunn, K. E., & Mulvenon, S. E. (2009). A critical review of research of formative assessment: The limited scientific evidence of the impact of formative assessment in education. *Practical Assessment, Research & Evaluation, 14*(7), 2–11.

Dunning, D., Heath, C., & Suls, J. M. (2004). Flawed self-assessment implications for health, education, and the workplace. *Psychological Science in the Public Interest, 5*(3), 69–106. doi:10.1111/j.1529-1006.2004.00018.x

Eastmond, D. (1995). *Alone but together: Adult distance study through computer conferencing.* Cresskill, NJ: Hampton Press.

Eddy, P., & Lawrence, A. (2013). Wikis as platforms for authentic assessment. *Innovative Higher Education, 38*(4), 253–265.

Edelstein, S., & Edwards, J. (2002). If you build it, they will come: Building learning communities through threaded discussions. *Online Journal of Distance Learning Administration 5*(1). Retrieved from http://www.westga.edu/~distance/ojdla/spring51/edelstein51.html

Edgar, B. D., & Willinsky, J. (2010). A survey of scholarly journals using Open Journal Systems. *Scholarly and Research Communication, 1*(2). Retrieved from http://www.src-online.ca/index.php/src/article/view/24/41

Eisner, E. W. (1994). *Educational imagination: On the design and evaluation of school programs* (3rd ed.). New York, NY: Macmillan.

Evans, T. & King, B. (1991). *Beyond the text: Contemporary writing on distance education.* Geelong, Australia: Deakin University Press.

Evans, T., & Nation, D. (Eds.). (1989). *Critical reflections on distance education.* London, UK: Falmer Press.

Feldstein, M., & Hill, P. (2016). Personalized learning: What it really is and why it really matters. *Educause Review, 51*(2), 25–35.

Fenwick, T. J., & Parsons, J. (2009). *The art of evaluation: A resource for educators and trainers* (2nd ed.). Toronto, ON: Thompson Educational Publishing.

Ferriman, J. (2013, July 11). How to prevent cheating in online courses [Blog post]. Retrieved from http://www.learndash.com/how-to-prevent-cheating-in-online-courses/

Freeman, S., Eddy, S. L., McDonough, M., Smith, M. K., Okoroafor, N., Jordt, H., & Wenderoth, M. P. (2014). Active learning increases student performance in science, engineering, and mathematics. *Proceedings of the National Academy of Sciences of the United States of America, 111*(23), 8410–8415. doi:10.1073/pnas.1319030111

Freire, P. (1970). *Pedagogy of the oppressed.* New York, NY: Continuum.

Friesen, N., & Wihak, C. (2013). From OER to PLAR: Credentialing for open education. *Open Praxis, 5*(1), 49–58. Retrieved from http://www.openpraxis.org/index.php/OpenPraxis/article/view/22/pdf

Gagne, R. (1971). Instruction based on research in learning. *Engineering Education, 61*(6), 519–523.

Garrison, D. R., & Akyol, Z. (2009). Role of instructional technology in the transformation of higher education. *Journal of Computing in Higher Education, 21*(1), 19–30.

Garrison, D. R., & Anderson, T. (2003). *E-learning in the 21st century: A framework for research and practice.* London: RoutledgeFalmer.

Garrison, D. R., Anderson, T., & Archer, W. (2000). Critical inquiry in a text-based environment: Computer conferencing in higher education. *The Internet and Higher Education, 2*(2–3), 87–105.

Garrison, D. R., & Archer, W. (2000). *A transactional perspective on teaching and learning: A framework for adult and higher education.* Amsterdam: Pergamon.

Garrison, D. R., & Cleveland-Innes, M. (2005). Facilitating cognitive presence in online learning: Interaction is not enough. *American Journal of Distance Education, 19*(3), 133–148. Retrieved from http://www.anitacrawley.net/Articles/GarrisonClevelandInnes2005.pdf

Garrison, D. R., & Vaughan, N. (2008). *Blended learning in higher education.* San Francisco, CA: Jossey-Bass.

Garrison, D. R., Cleveland-Innes, M., & Vaughan, N. (n.d.). *The Community of Inquiry.* Retrieved from https://coi.athabascau.ca/

Garton, L., Haythornthwaite, C., & Wellman, B. (1997). Studying online social networks. *Journal of Computer-Mediated Communication, 3*(1). Retrieved from http://jcmc.huji.ac.il/vol3/issue1/garton.html

George, B., Sims, P., McLean, A.N., & Mayer, D. (2011). Discovering your authentic leadership. In *HBR's 10 must reads on leadership* (pp. 163–177). Boston, MA: Harvard Business School Publishing.

Gibbs, G. (2010). *Dimensions of quality.* York, UK: The Higher Education Academy. Retrieved from https://www.heacademy.ac.uk/sites/default/files/dimensions_of_quality.pdf

Ginsberg, G. (2015, December 4). What a college student looks like. *Maclean's.* Retrieved from http://www.macleans.ca/education/what-a-college-student-looks-like/

Gipps, C., & Stobart, G. (2009). Fairness in assessment. In C. Wyatt-Smith & J. J. Cumming (Eds.), *Education assessment in the 21st century: Connecting theory and practice* (pp. 105–118). Netherlands: Springer.

Godin, S. (2016, June 1). Read more blogs. *Seth's Blog.* Retrieved from http://sethgodin.typepad.com/seths_blog/2016/06/read-more-blogs.html

Goff, L., Potter, M. K., Pierre, E., Carey, T., Gullage, A., Kustra, E., . . .& Van Gastel, G. (2015). *Learning outcomes assessment: A practitioner's handbook.* Toronto, ON: Higher Education Quality Council of Ontario. Retrieved from http://www.heqco.ca/SiteCollectionDocuments/heqco.LOAhandbook_Eng_2015.pdf

Goffman, E. (1959). *The presentation of self in everyday life.* Garden City, NJ: Doubleday.

Gulikers, J. M., Bastiaens, T. J., & Kirschner, P. A. (2004). A five-dimensional framework for authentic assessment. *Educational Technology Research and Development, 52*(3), 67–86.

Gunawardena, C. N. (1995). Social presence theory and implications for interaction and collaborative learning in computer conferences. *International Journal of Educational Telecommunications, 1*(2/3), 147–166.

Gunawardena, C. N., & Zittle, F. (1997). Social presence as a predictor of satisfaction within a computer-mediated conferencing environment. *American Journal of Distance Education, 11*(3), 8–26.

Guri-Rosenblit, S. (2014). Distance education systems and institutions in the online era: An identity crisis. In O. Zawacki-Richter & T. Anderson (Eds.), *Online distance education: Towards a research agenda* (pp. 109–130). Edmonton, AB: Athabasca University Press.

Hake, R. R. (1998). Interactive-engagement versus traditional methods: A six-thousand-student survey of mechanics. *American Journal of Physics, 66*(1), 64–74.

Harmon, J., & Copeland, A. (2016). Students' perceptions of digital badges in a public library management course. *Education for Information, 32*(1), 87–100. doi:10.3233/EFI-150964

Harrison, J. B., & West, R. E. (2014). Sense of community in a blended technology integration course: A design-based research study. *International Review of Research in Open and Distributed Learning, 15*(6). Retrieved from http://www.irrodl.org/index.php/irrodl/article/view/1907/3129

Hart, K. (2013). Some historical notes on the decline of the universities. *Anthropologies: A collaborative online project.* Retrieved from www.anthropologiesproject.org/2013

Haskins, C. H. (1957). *The rise of universities.* Ithaca, NY: Cornell University Press.

Hattie, J., & Timperley, H. (2007). The power of feedback. *Review of Educational Research, 77*(1), 81–112.

Hensiek, S., DeKorver, B. K., Harwood, C. J., Fish, J., O Shea, K., & Towns, M. (2017). Digital badges in science: A novel approach to the assessment of student learning. *Journal of College Science Teaching, 46*(3), 28–33.

Herrington, J., Oliver, R., & Reeves, T. C. (2006). Authentic tasks online: A synergy among learner, task and technology. *Distance Education, 27*(2), 233–248.

Higher Education Quality Council of Ontario. (2015). Research. Retrieved from http://www.heqco.ca/en-ca/Research/Pages/Home.aspx

Hill, P. (2016, 24 May). Distance ed's second act. *Chronicle of Higher Education.* Retrieved from http://chronicle.com/article/Distance-Ed-s-Second-Act/236571

Hill, P., & Barber, M. (2014). *Preparing for a renaissance in assessment.* London, UK: Pearson. Retrieved from http://gr8dbl.doverbay.ca/wp-content/uploads/2015/04/Preparing_for_a_Renaissance_in_assessment.pdf

Hiltz, S. R., & Turoff, M. (2005). Education goes digital: The evolution of online learning and the revolution in higher education. *Communications of the ACM, 48*(10), 59–64.

Hiltz, S., Shen, J., & Swan, K. (2006). Assessment and collaboration in online learning. *Journal of Asynchronous Learning Networks, 10*(1), 45–62. Retrieved from http://go.galegroup.com/ps/i.do?id=GALE%7CA284325461&v=2.1&u=atha49011&it=r&p=AONE&sw=w&asid=73565e3b6168c26a8ed6f89bd5570144

Holmberg, B. (1986). *Growth and structure of distance education* (3rd ed.). London, UK: Croom Helm.

Holmen, M. (2014, August 6). Education vs. learning–What exactly is the difference? *EdTechReview.* Retrieved from http://edtechreview.in/trends-insights/insights/1417-education-vs-learning-what-exactly-is-the-difference

Horn, M., & Staker, H. (2012, November 14). Formative assessment is foundational to blended learning. *The Journal*. Retrieved from http://thejournal.com/articles/2012/11/14/formative-assessment-is-foundational-to-blended-learning.aspx

Hossenfelder, S. (2016, August 11). What I learned as a hired consultant to autodidact physicists. *Aeon*. Retrieved from https://aeon.co/ideas/what-i-learned-as-a-hired-consultant-for-autodidact-physicists

Houle, C. (1960). *The inquiring mind*. Madison: University of Wisconsin Press.

Jarvis, P. (2010). *Adult education and lifelong education: Theory and practice* (4th ed.). London, UK: Routledge.

Jensen, J. L., Kummer, T. A., & Godoy, P. D. d. M. (2015). Improvements from a flipped classroom may simply be the fruits of active learning. *CBE Life Sciences Education, 14*(1), art. 5. http://doi.org/10.1187/cbe.14-08-0129

Jeong, A. (2007). The effects of intellectual openness and gender on critical thinking processes in computer-supported collaborative argumentation. *Journal of Distance Education, 22*(1), 1–18.

JISC. (2010). *Effective assessment in a digital age: A guide to technology-enhanced assessment and feedback*. Retrieved from http://www.webarchive.org.uk/wayback/archive/20140614115719/http://www.jisc.ac.uk/media/documents/programmes/elearning/digiassass_eada.pdf

Jones, C. (2005). Who are you? Theorizing from the experience of working through an avatar. *E-learning, 2*(4), 414–425.

Junco, R., Heiberger, G., & Loken, E. (2011). The effect of Twitter on college student engagement and grades. *Journal of Computer Assisted Learning, 27*(2), 119–132.

Kasworm, C., Rose, A., & Ross-Gordon, J. (2010). *Handbook of adult and continuing education*. Thousand Oaks, CA: Sage.

Kay, K., & Greenhill, V. (2011). Twenty-first century students need 21st century skills. In G. Wan & D. M. Gut (Eds.), *Bringing schools into the 21st century* (pp. 41–65). New York, NY: Springer.

Kayler, M., & Weller, K. (2007). Pedagogy, self-assessment, and online discussion groups. *Educational Technology & Society, 10*(1), 136–147. Retrieved from http://www.ifets.info/journals/10_1/13.pdf

Keegan, D. (2005). Reintegration of the teaching acts. In D. Keegan (Ed.), *Theoretical principles of distance education* (pp. 113–134). London: Taylor & Francis e-Library.

Kelly, R. (2009, January 19). Transformative learning: Q&A with Patricia Cranton. Retrieved from http://www.facultyfocus.com/articles/instructional-design/transformative-learning-qa-with-patricia-cranton/

Kenny, N. (2011, March 11). How do you write a program-level learning outcome? [Blog post]. Retrieved from https://natashakenny.wordpress.com/page/3/

Kirschner, P., Strijbos, J-W., & Kreijns, K. (2004). Designing integrated, collaborative e-learning. In W. Jochems, J. van Merrienboer, & R. Koper (Eds.), *Integrated e-learning: Implications for pedagogy, technology & organization* (pp. 24–38). London: RoutledgeFalmer.

Knowles, M. (1970). *The modern practice of adult education: Andragogy versus pedagogy.* Chicago, IL: Follett.

Ko, S., & Rossen, S. (2010). *Teaching online: A practical guide* (3rd Ed.). London: Routledge.

Kollar, I., & Fischer, F. (2010). Peer assessment as collaborative learning: A cognitive perspective. *Learning and instruction: Unravelling peer assessment, 20*(4), 344–348. doi:10.1016/j.learninstruc.2009.08.005

Kolowich, S. (2014, July 10). Can MOOCs help professors teach traditional courses more effectively? [Blog post]. *Chronicle of Higher Education.* Retrieved from https://www.chronicle.com/blogs/wiredcampus/can-moocs-help-professors-teach-traditional-courses-more-efficiently/53851

Kristof, N. (2014, February 15). Professors, we need you! *New York Times.* Retrieved from http://www.nytimes.com/2014/02/16/opinion/sunday/kristof-professors-we-need-you.html

Kupczynski, L., Ice, P., Wiesenmayer, R., & McCluskey, F. (2010). Student perceptions of the relationship between indicators of teaching and success in online courses. *Journal of Interactive Online Learning, 9*(1), 23–43. Retrieved from http://www.ncolr.org/jiol/issues/pdf/9.1.2.pdf

Lange, E. (2006). Challenging social philosophobia. In T. Fenwick, T. Nesbit, & B. Spencer (Eds.), *Contexts of adult education: Canadian perspectives* (pp. 92–104). Toronto, ON: Thompson.

Lantz, M. (2010). The use of clickers in the classroom: Teaching innovation or merely an amusing novelty? *Computers in Human Behavior, 26*(4), 556–561.

Larsen, R. (2009). *The selected works of T. S. Spivet.* New York, NY: Penguin.

Latchem, C. (2014). Quality assurance in online distance education. In O. Zawacki-Richter & T. Anderson (Eds.), *Online distance education; Towards a research agenda* (pp. 311–341). Edmonton, AB: Athabasca University Press.

Laurillard, D. (2012). *Teaching as a design science: Building pedagogical patterns for learning and technology.* New York, NY: Routledge.

Lee, S. J., Srinivasan, S., Trail, T., Lewis, D., & Lopez, S. (2011). Examining the relationship among student perception of support, course satisfaction, and learning outcomes in online learning. *Internet and Higher Education, 14*(3), 158–163.

Lehman, R., & Conceição, S. C. (2011). *Creating a sense of presence in online teaching: How to "be there" for distance learners*. San Francisco, CA: Jossey-Bass.

Liang, J-C., & Tsai, C-C. (2008). Internet self-efficacy and preferences toward constructivist internet-based learning environments: A study of pre-school teachers in Taiwan. *Educational Technology & Society, 11*(1), 226–237.

Lindeman, E. (1926). *The meaning of adult education*. New York, NY: New Republic.

Lindstrom, G., & Dyjur, P. (2017). From student to instructor: Reflections on receiving and issuing digital badges for educational development. *Transformative Dialogues: Teaching & Learning Journal, 9*(3), 1–4.

Mackeracher, D. (2004). *Making sense of adult learning* (2nd ed.). Toronto, ON: University of Toronto Press.

Mager, R. F. (1997). *Preparing instructional objectives: A critical tool in the development of effective instruction* (3rd ed.). Atlanta, GA: CEP Press.

Magro, K. (2001). Perspectives and theories of adult learning. In D. Poonwassie & A. Poonwassie (Eds.), *Fundamentals of adult education: Foundations, practices, issues* (pp. 76–97). Toronto, ON: Thompson.

Mah, D. (2016). Learning analytics and digital badges: Potential impact on student retention in higher education. *Technology, Knowledge & Learning, 21*(3), 285–305. doi:10.1007/s10758-016-9286-8

Mansouri, S. A., & Piki, A. (2016). An exploration into the impact of blogs on students' learning: Case studies in postgraduate business education. *Innovations in Education & Teaching International, 53*(3), 260–273. doi:10.1080/14703297.2014.997777

Mathur, S., & Murray, T. (2006). Authentic assessment online: A practical and theoretical challenge in higher education. In D. Williams, S. Howell, & M. Hricko (Eds.), *Online assessment, measurement and evaluation: Emerging practices* (pp. 238–258). Hershey, PA: Idea Group.

Matuga, J. M. (2006). The role of assessment and evaluation in context: Pedagogical alignment, constraints, and affordances in online courses. In D. D. Williams, S. L. Howell, & M. Hricko (Eds.), *Online assessment, measure and evaluation: Emerging practices* (pp. 316–330). Hershey, PA: Idea Group.

Mayes, T. (2006). Theoretical perspectives on interactivity in e-learning. In C. Juwah (Ed.), *Interactions in online education: Implications for theory and practice* (pp. 9–26). London: Routledge.

Mbati, L. (2013). Online social media applications for constructivism and observational learning. *International Review of Research in Open and Distributed Learning, 14*(5). Retrieved from http://www.irrodl.org/index.php/irrodl/article/view/1579

McDaniel, R. (2016). A taxonomy for digital badge design in medical technologies. 2016 IEEE International Conference on Serious Games and Applications for Health (SeGAH). doi:10.1109/SeGAH.2016.7586254

McElhone, R. (2015). Blended learning: What's all the fuss about? [*b online learning* blog post]. Retrieved from https://bonlinelearning.com.au/blog/blended-learning-whats-all-the-fuss-about/

McKeachie, W. J., Pintrich, P. R., Lin, Y., & Smith, D. A. F. (1987). *Teaching and learning in the college classroom: A review of the research literature.* Ann Arbor, MI: National Center for Research to Improve Postsecondary Teaching and Learning.

McLoughlin, C., & Oliver, R. (2000). Designing learning environments for cultural inclusivity: A case study of indigenous online learning at tertiary level. *Australian Journal of Educational Technology, 16*(1), 58–72. Retrieved from http://www.ascilite.org.au/ajet/ajet16/mcloughlin.html

Medland, E. (2010). Reconceptualising subjectivity in assessment. Paper presented at the Society for Research into Higher Education (SRHE) Annual Conference, Newport, Wales. Retrieved from http://www.srhe.ac.uk/conference2010/abstracts/0200.pdf

Mezirow, J. (1997, Summer). Transformative learning: Theory to practice. *New Directions for Adult and Continuing Education, 74,* 5–12.

Michael, J. (2006). Where's the evidence that active learning works? *Advances in Physiology Education, 30*(4), 159–167.

Moebs, S. (2013). Blended learning for learners in SMEs. In N. P. Ololube (Ed.), *Advancing technology and educational development through blended learning in emerging economies* (pp. 36–58). Hershey, PA: IGI Global.

Moon, T. R., Brighton, C. M., Callahan, C. M., & Robinson, A. (2005). Development Of authentic assessments for the middle school classroom. *Journal of Secondary Gifted Education, 16*(2–3), 119–135.

Moore, J. L., Dickson-Deane, C., & Galyen, K. (2011). e-Learning, online learning, and distance learning environments: Are they the same? *The Internet and Higher Education, 14,* 129–135. doi:10.1016/j.iheduc.2010.10.001

Moore, J. L., Rosinski, P., Peeples, T., Pigg, S., Rife, M. C., Brunk-Chavez, B., . . . Grabill, J. T. (2016). Revisualizing composition: How first-year writers use composing technologies. *Computers & Composition, 39,* 1–13. doi:10.1016/j.compcom.2015.11.001

Moore, M. G. (1973). Towards a theory of independent learning and teaching. *Journal of Higher Education, 44*(12), 661–679. Retrieved from http://192.107.92.31/Corsi_2005/bibliografia%20e-learning/theory.pdf

Moore, M. G. (1989). Three modes of interaction. A presentation of the NUCEA forum: Issues in instructional interactivity. *NUCEA Conference,* Salt Lake City, UT.

Moore, M. G. (1993). Theory of transactional distance. In D. Keegan (Ed.), *Theoretical principles of distance education* (pp. 22–38). New York: Routledge.

Moore, M. G., & Kearsley, G. (2005). *Distance education: A systems view* (2nd ed.). Belmont, CA: Wadsworth Cengage.

Morrison, D. (2007). E-learning in higher education: The need for a new pedagogy. In M. Bullen & D. James (Eds.), *Making the transition to e-learning: Strategies and issues* (pp. 104–120). Hersey, PA: Information Science Publishing.

Mozilla Foundation. (n.d.). Open badges. Retrieved from https://openbadges.org/about/

Nagel, L., & Kotzé, T. G. (2010). Supersizing e-learning: What a CoI survey reveals about teaching presence in a large online class. *The Internet and Higher Education, 13*(1–2), 45–51. doi:10.1016/j.iheduc.2009.12.001

Neal, E. (n.d.). Assessment of student learning in STEM disciplines. A Duke University "Teaching IDEAS" workshop. Durham, NC.

Newman, A. (2015). Evidence of learning: A framework for facilitation. *Educause Review, 50*(6), 46–62.

Newton, D. (2015). The (accidental) power of MOOCs. *The Atlantic.* Retrieved from https://www.theatlantic.com/education/archive/2015/06/the-secret-power-of-moocs/396608/

Nonaka, I. (1994). A dynamic theory of organizational knowledge creation. *Organizational Science, 5*(1), 14–37.

Northcutt, C. G., Ho, A. D., & Chuang, I. L. (2016). Detecting and preventing "multiple-account" cheating in MOOCs. *Computers and Education, 100*(C), 71–80. Retrieved from http://arxiv.org/abs/1508.05699

OCW Consortium Global Conference. (2014). Conference schedule. Retrieved from http://conference.ocwconsortium.org/2014/schedule/

Ontario Ministry of Advanced Education and Skills Development. (2015, December 1). Essential Employability Skills. Retrieved from http://www.tcu.gov.on.ca/pepg/audiences/colleges/progstan/essential.html

OntarioLearn. (2011). Module III – Assessment and Evaluation. Retrieved from http://ontariolearn.com/facultyteachingresources/ModIII.html

Openo, J., Laverty, C., Klodiana, K., Borin, P., Goff, L., Stranach, M., & Gomaa, N. (2017). Bridging the divide: Leveraging the scholarship of teaching and learning for quality enhancement. *Canadian Journal for the Scholarship of Teaching and Learning, 8*(2). Retrieved from http://ir.lib.uwo.ca/cjsotl_rcacea/vol8/iss2/6

Openo, J. (2017, June). *You can fast forward your instructor: An interpretive phenomenological analysis of blended learning.* Paper presented at Society for Teaching in Learning in Higher Education, Halifax, NS.

Palahicky, S. G. (2017). *A description of a successful Indigenous online high school: Perspectives of teachers, staff, students, and parents* (Unpublished doctoral dissertation). Athabasca University, Athabasca, AB. Retrieved from http://hdl. handle.net/10791/219

Paulin, D., & Gilbert, S. (2016). Social media and learning. In C. Haythornthwaite, R. Andrews, J. Fransman, & E. M. Meyers (Eds.), *The Sage handbook of e-learning research* (pp. 354–374). Los Angeles, CA: Sage.

Piaget, J. (1972). Intellectual evolution from adolescence to adulthood. *Human Development, 15,* 1–12.

Plumb, D., & Welton, M. 2001. Theory building in adult education: Questioning our grasp of the obvious. In D. Poonwassie & A. Poonwassie (Eds.), *Fundamentals of adult education: Foundations, practices, issues* (pp. 63–75). Toronto, ON: Thompson.

Poe, M., & Stassen, M. (Eds.). (n.d.). *Teaching and learning online: Communication, community, and assessment.* A Handbook for UMass Faculty. University of Massachusetts. Retrieved from http://www.umass.edu/oapa/ oapa/publications/online_handbooks/Teaching_and_Learning_Online_ Handbook.pdf

Polanyi, M. (1966). *The tacit dimension.* London: Routledge and Kegan Paul.

Pratt, D. (2005). Teaching. In L. English (Ed.), *International encyclopedia of adult education* (pp. 610–615). New York: Palgrave Macmillan.

Pratt, D. D. (1981). The dynamics of continuing education learning groups. *Canadian Journal of University Continuing Education, 8*(1), 26–32.

Prince, M. (2004). Does active learning work? A review of the research. *Journal of Engineering Education, 93*(3), 223–231.

Prinsloo, P. (2017, June 2). (De)constructing [online]* learning: Salvation, stigma and/or snake oil. Keynote address at the Learning Carnival – Celebrating Innovation and Excellence in Teaching and Learning. North-West University, Mahikeng, South Africa. Retrieved from https://www.slideshare.net/prinsp/ deconstructing-online-learning-salvation-stigma-andor-snake-oil

Prior Learning Centre. (n.d). Retrieved from http://www.priorlearning.ca/

Purkey, W. (1992). An introduction to invitational theory. *Journal of Invitational Theory and Practice, 1*(1), 5–16.

Race, P. (2001). *The lecturer's toolkit: A practical guide to teaching, learning and assessment.* London, UK: Kogan Page.

Ramsden, P. (1992). *Learning to teach in higher education.* London, UK: Routledge.

Ravenscroft, A. (2011). Dialogue and connectivism: A new approach to understanding and promoting dialogue-rich networked learning. *International*

Review of Research in Open and Distributed Learning, 12(3). Retrieved from http://www.irrodl.org/index.php/irrodl/article/view/934

Rees, J. (2015, September 18). Somebody's gotta do it. [*Chronicle Vitae* blog post]. Retrieved from https://chroniclevitae.com/news/1127-somebody-s-gotta-do-it

Reeves, T., Herrington, J., & Oliver, R. (2002). Authentic activities and online learning. In *Quality Conversations, Proceedings of the 25th HERDSA Annual Conference, Perth, Western Australia, 7–10 July 2002* (pp. 562–567). Retrieved from http://ro.ecu.edu.au/ecuworks/3900/

Reigeluth, C. (2012). Instructional theory and technology for the new paradigm of education. *RED, Revista de Educación a distancia, 32*, 1–18. Retrieved from www.redalyc.org/pdf/547/54724591002.pdf

Renner, P. (1993). *The art of teaching adults: How to become an exceptional instructor and facilitator.* Vancouver, BC: Training Associates.

Roberts, T., & McInnerney, J. (2007). Seven problems of online group learning (and their solutions). *International Forum of Educational Technology & Society, 10*(4), 257–268.

Rogers, C. R. (1969). *Freedom to learn.* Columbus, OH: Charles E. Merrill.

Rohr, L., & Costello, J. (2015). Student perceptions of Twitter's effectiveness for assessment in a large enrollment online course. *Online Learning, 19*(4). Retrieved from https://olj.onlinelearningconsortium.org/index.php/olj/article/viewFile/540/167

Rohr, L. E., Costello, J., & Hawkins, T. (2015). Design considerations for integrating Twitter into an online course. *International Review of Research in Open and Distributed Learning, 16*(4). Retrieved from http://www.irrodl.org/index.php/irrodl/article/view/1078

Roscorla, T. (2014, July 16). A critical look at blended learning. *Converge.* Center for Digital Education. Retrieved from http://www.centerdigitaled.com/news/A-Critical-Look-at-Blended-Learning.html

Rose, E. (2013). *On reflection: An essay on technology, education, and the status of thought in the twenty-first century.* Toronto, ON: Canadian Scholars' Press.

Ross, J., Gallagher, M. S., & Macleod, H. (2013). Making distance visible: Assembling nearness in an online distance learning programme. *International Review of Open and Distributed Learning, 14*(4). Retrieved from http://www.irrodl.org/index.php/irrodl/issue/view/58

Rovai, A. F. (2002). Building sense of community at a distance. *International Review of Open and Distributed Learning, 3*(1). Retrieved from http://www.irrodl.org/index.php/irrodl/article/view/79/152

Rovai, A. F., & Jordan, H. (2004). Blended learning and sense of community: A comparative analysis with traditional and fully online graduate course.

International Review of Research in Open and Distributed Learning, 13(1). Retrieved from http://www.irrodl.org/index.php/irrodl/article/view/192

Rowntree, D. (1977). *Assessing students: How shall we know them?* London, UK: Harper & Row.

Rust, C., O'Donovan, B., & Price, M. (2005). A social constructivist assessment process model: How the research literature shows us this could be best practice. *Assessment & Evaluation in Higher Education, 30*(3), 231–240. doi: 10.1080/02602930500063819

Saba, F. (2014, March). Introduction to distance education: Theorists and theories: Otto Peters. *Distance-educator.com*. Retrieved from http://distance-educator.com/introduction-to-distance-education-theorists-and-theories-otto-peters/

Salomon, G., & Perkins, D. N. (1989). Rocky roads to transfer: Rethinking mechanism of a neglected phenomenon. *Educational Psychologist, 24*(2), 113.

Sands, A. (2014, May 25). Essay-marking software gives high marks for gibberish, U.S. expert warns. *Edmonton Journal*. Retrieved from http://www.edmontonjournal.com/Essay+marking+software+gives+high+marks+gibberish+expert+warns+Alberta/9874562/story.html

Schön, D. (1983). *The reflective practitioner: How professionals think in action*. New York, NY: Basic Books.

Schwier, R. (2007). Shaping the metaphor of community in online environments. In G. Calverley, M. Childs, & L. Schneiders (Eds.), *Video for education* (pp. 68–76). London, UK: DIVERSE and the Association for Learning Technologies.

Scott, S. M. (2006). A way of seeing: Transformation for a new century. In T. Fenwick, T. Nesbit, & B. Spencer (Eds.), *Contexts of adult education: Canadian perspectives* (pp. 151–161). Toronto, ON: Thompson.

Selman, G., (2001). Stages in the development of adult education. In D. H. Poonwassie, & A. Poonwassie (Eds.), *Fundamentals of adult education: Issues and practices for lifelong learning* (pp. 31-43). Toronto, ON: Thompson.

Selman, G., & Dampier, P. (1991). *The foundations of adult education in Canada*. Toronto, ON: Thompson.

Selman, G. M., Cooke, M., Selman, M., & Dampier, P. (1998). *The foundations of adult education in Canada*. (2nd.ed.). Toronto, ON: Thompson.

Selznick, P. (1996). In search of community. In W. Vitek & W. Jackson (Eds.), *Rooted in the land: Essays on community and place* (pp. 195–203). New Haven, CT: Yale University Press.

Shackelford, J. L., & Maxwell, M. (2012). Sense of community in graduate online education: Contribution of learner to learner interaction. *International Review of Open and Distributed Learning, 13*(4). Retrieved from http://www.irrodl.org/index.php/irrodl/issue/view/53

Shea, C. (2014, April 14). The new academic celebrity. *Chronicle of Higher Education*. Retrieved from http://chronicle.com/article/The-New-Academic-Celebrity/145845?ci

Shih, L., & Swan, K. (2005). Fostering social presence in asynchronous online class discussions. *Proceedings of the 2005 conference on Computer Support for Collaborative Learning* (pp. 602–606).

Shimamoto, D. (2012). Implementing a flipped classroom: An instructional module. Paper presented at Technology, Colleges, and Community Worldwide Online Conference. http://scholarspace.manoa.hawaii.edu/handle/10125/22527

Shirky, C. (2009, June). How social media can make history. [Video File]. *Ted*. Retrieved from https://www.ted.com/talks/clay_shirky_how_cellphones_twitter_facebook_can_make_history

Siemens, G. (2005). Connectivism: A learning theory for the digital age. *International Journal of Instructional Technology Distance Learning, 2*(1), 3–10.

Siemens, G., & Conole, G. (2011). Editorial. Connectivism: Design and delivery of social networked learning. *International Review of Research in Open and Distributed Learning, 12*(3). Retrieved from http://www.irrodl.org/index.php/irrodl/article/view/994/1820

Simonson, M., Smaldino, S., Albright, A., & Zvacek, S. (2012). *Teaching and learning at a distance: Foundations of distance education* (5th ed.). Boston, MA: Pearson.

Singer, D. L., Astrachan, B. M., Gould., L. J., & Klein, E. B. (1975). Boundary management in psychological work with groups. *Journal of Applied Behavioural Science, 11*(2), 137–176.

Snyder, M. (1987). *Public appearances/private realities: The psychology of self-monitoring,* New York, NY: W. H. Freeman and Company.

Spencer, B. (1998). *The purposes of adult education: A guide for students*. Toronto, ON: Thompson.

Spencer, B. (2004). Online adult learning. In G. Foley (Ed.), *Dimensions of adult learning: Adult education and training in a global era* (pp. 189–200). Berkshire, UK: Open University Press.

Stacey, E. (1999). Collaborative learning in an online environment. *Journal of Distance Education, 14*(2), 14–33.

Stanford History Education Group. (n.d.). Constructivism: Actively building knowledge. Retrieved from http://teachinghistory.org/teaching-materials/ask-a-master-teacher/23896

Steinke, P., & Fitch, P. (2007, Summer). Assessing service-learning. *Research and Practice in Assessment, 2*, 24–29. Retrieved from http://www.rpajournal.com/dev/wp-content/uploads/2012/05/A32.pdf

Stetson-Tiligadas, S. M. (2017). *The impact of digital achievement badges on undergraduate learner motivation* (Unpublished doctoral dissertation). Capella University, Minneapolis, MN. Retrieved from ProQuest Dissertations. (10037460)

Sullivan, F. M. (2013). New and alternative assessments, digital badges, and civics: An overview of emerging themes and promising directions. CIRCLE Working Paper #77. Retrieved from https://civicyouth.org/wp-content/uploads/2013/03/WP_77_Sullivan_Final.pdf

Swan, K. (2002). Building communities in online courses: The importance of interaction. *Education, Communication and Information, 2*(1), 23–49.

Swan, K., Schenker, J., Arnold, S., & Kuo, C-L. (2007). Shaping online discussion: Assessment matters. *e-mentor, 1*(18), 78–82. Retrieved from http://www.e-mentor.edu.pl/mobi/artykul/index/numer/18/id/390

Travers, N., Smith, B., Ellis, L., Brady, T., Feldman, L., Hakim, K., . . . Treadwell, A. (2011). Language of evaluation: How PLA evaluators write about student learning. *International Review of Research in Open and Distributed Learning, 12*(1), 80–95. Retrieved from http://www.irrodl.org/index.php/irrodl/article/view/946.

Tuckman, B.W. (1965). Developmental sequence in small groups. *Psychological Bulletin, 63*(7), 384–399.

Turkle, S. (1997). *Life on the screen: Identity in the age of the Internet.* London, UK: Phoenix.

University of Reading. (n.d.). Engage in assessment. Retrieved from https://www.reading.ac.uk/engageinassessment/

University of Wisconsin–Eau Claire. (n.d.). Service-learning. Retrieved from www.uwec.edu/SL/students/examples.htm

Varsavsky, C., & Rayner, G. (2013). Strategies that challenge: Exploring the use of differentiated assessment to challenge high-achieving students in large enrolment undergraduate cohorts. *Assessment & Evaluation in Higher Education, 38*(7), 789–802.

Vaughan, N. D., Cleveland-Innes, M., & Garrison, D. R. (2013). *Teaching in blended learning environments: Creating and sustaining communities of inquiry.* Edmonton, AB: Athabasca University Press. Retrieved from http://www.aupress.ca/books/120229/ebook/99Z_Vaughan_et_al_2013-Teaching_in_Blended_Learning_Environments.pdf

Veletsianos, G., & Navarrete, C. (2012). Online social networks as formal learning environments: Learner experiences and activities. *International Review of*

Research in Open and Distributed Learning, 13(1). Retrieved from http://www.irrodl.org/index.php/irrodl/article/view/1078

Vygotsky, L. (1978). *Mind in society: The development of higher psychological processes.* Cambridge, MA: Harvard University Press.

Wagner, E. (1997). Interactivity: From agents to outcome. In T. E. Cyrs (Ed.), *Teaching and learning at a distance: What it takes to effectively design, deliver, and evaluate programs* (pp. 19–26). San Francisco, CA: Jossey-Bass.

Wall, A. F., Hursh, D., & Rodgers, J. W. (2014). Assessment for whom: Repositioning higher education assessment as an ethical and value-focused social practice. *Research & Practice in Assessment, 9*(1), 5–13. Retrieved from www.rpajournal.com/dev/wp-content/uploads/2014/06/SF.pdf

Walvoord, B. E. (2010). *Assessment clear and simple: A practical guide for institutions, departments, and general education.* San Francisco, CA: Jossey-Bass.

Wang, Z., Chen, L., & Anderson, T. (2014). A framework for interaction and cognitive engagement in connectivist learning contexts. *International Review of Research in Open and Distributed Learning, 15*(2). Retrieved from http://www.irrodl.org/index.php/irrodl/article/view/1709

Webb, M., & Gibson, D. (2015). Technology enhanced assessment in complex collaborative settings. *Education & Information Technologies, 20*(4), 675–695. doi:10.1007/s10639-015-9413-5

Webb, N. (1994). *Group collaboration in assessment: Competing objectives, processes, and outcomes.* CSE Technical Report 386. Retrieved from https://cresst.org/wp-content/uploads/TECH386.pdf

Webb, N. J., & Grib, T. F. (1967). Teaching process as a learning experience: The experimental use of student-led discussion groups. West de Pere, WI: Saint Norbert College. Retrieved from https://files.eric.ed.gov/fulltext/ED019708.pdf

Webber, K. L. (2012). The use of learner-centered assessment in US colleges and universities. *Research in Higher Education, 53*(2), 201–228. doi:10.1007/s11162-011-9245-0

Wegerif, R. (1998). The social dimension of asynchronous learning networks. *Journal of Asynchronous Learning Networks, 2*(1). Retrieved from https://www.researchgate.net/profile/Rupert_Wegerif/publication/228598781_The_Social_Dimension_of_Asynchronous_Learning_Networks/links/09e415124c0b8ebadf000000.pdf

Weller, M. (2011). *The digital scholar: How technology is transforming scholarly practice.* London, UK: Bloomsbury Academic. Retrieved from https://www.bloomsburycollections.com/book/the-digital-scholar-how-technology-is-transforming-scholarly-practice/

Wenger, E. (1998). *Communities of practice: Learning, meaning and identity.* New York, NY: Cambridge University Press.

White, S., Davis, A., Dickens, K., León, M., & Sanchez-Vera, M. (2015). MOOCs: What motivates the providers and the participants? In S. Zvacek, M. Restivo, J. Uhomoibhi & M. Helfert (Eds.), *Computer supported education* (pp. 99–104). 6th International Conference, CSEDU 2014. Revised Selected Papers. Switzerland: Springer.

Wiley, D. (2017). Iterating toward openness: Lessons learned on a personal journey. In R. S Jhangiani & R. Biswas-Diener (Eds.), *Open: The philosophy and practices that are revolutionizing education and science* (pp. 195–207). London: Ubiquity Press. doi:10.5334/bbc.o.

Wiliam, D. (2006). Formative assessment: Getting the focus right. *Educational Assessment, 11*(3–4), 283–289.

Wilson, B. G., Ludwig-Hardman, S., Thornam, C. L., & Dunlap, J. C. (2004). Bounded community: Designing and facilitating learning communities in formal courses. *International Review of Research in Open and Distributed Learning, 5*(3). Retrieved from http://www.irrodl.org/index.php/irrodl/article/view/204

Windham, C. (2007). Why today's students value authentic learning. Educause Learning Initiative, Paper No. 9. Retrieved from https://www.educause.edu/ir/library/pdf/ELI3017.pdf

Wisneski, J. E., Ozogul, G., & Bichelmeyer, B. A. (2015). Does teaching presence transfer between MBA teaching environments? A comparative investigation of instructional design practices associated with teaching presence. *The Internet and Higher Education, 25*, 18–27. doi:10.1016/j.iheduc.2014.11.001

Wittmann-Price, R., & Godshall, M. (2009). Strategies to promote deep learning in clinical nursing courses. *Nurse Educator, 34*(5), 214–216. doi:10.1097/NNE.0b013e3181b2b576

Wlodkowski, R. (1999). *Enhancing adult motivation to learn: A comprehensive guide for teaching all adults* (2nd ed.). San Francisco, CA: Jossey-Bass.

Wlodkowski, R. (2008). *Enhancing adult motivation to learn: A comprehensive guide for teaching all adults* (3rd ed.). San Francisco, CA: Jossey-Bass.

Yang, J. C., Quadir, B., & Chen, N. (2016). Effects of the badge mechanism on self-efficacy and learning performance in a game-based English learning environment. *Journal of Educational Computing Research, 54*(3), 371–394. doi:10.1177/0735633115620433

Yang, Y-F, Yeh, H-C., & Wong, W-K. (2010). The influence of social interaction on meaning construction in a virtual community. *British Journal of Educational Technology, 41*(2), 287–306.

Young, J. R. (2012, August 16). Dozens of plagiarism incidents are reported in Coursera's free online courses. *Chronicle of Higher Education*. Retrieved from http://chronicle.com/article/Dozens-of-PlagiarismIncidents/133697

Zimmerman, D. (2013). Working smarter, not harder: Building independent communities of practice. In A. L. Costa & P. W. O'Leary (Eds.). *The power of the social brain: Teaching, learning, and interdependent thinking.* (pp. 84–93). Columbia, NY: Teachers College Press.

Zinn, L. (1990). Identifying your philosophical orientation. In M. W. Galbraith (Ed.), *Adult learning methods: A guide to effective instruction* (pp. 37–72). Malabar, FL: Krieger.

Index

MOOCs. *See* Massive Open Online Courses
multimedia, 28, 47

online learning: definition, 8; history, 21
Ontario Quality Assurance Framework, 20
open access, 105: assessment in, 105
Open and Distributed Learning (ODL), 8, 48
open assessments, 161
Open Education Resources (OER), 93–95, 147
open movement, 95, 97, 104–105
outcomes: expressive, 108; learning, 5–6, 18, 20, 35, 62–66, 76, 81, 103, 108–109, 111–112, 116, 122, 151, 168

participation, 10, 22, 29, 32, 47–48, 96, 114–115, 118–119, 122–123, 125, 128, 130, 141, 149, 164–165: assessment of, 123, 164–165
peer assessment, 57, 69, 86, 95–96, 147, 149, 154, 161
peer review, 97–98, 135, 138
Perry, Beth, 167, 169
philosophy: of control, 51; overview of, 38
portfolios, 48, 73, 75, 78–79, 135, 151, 161, 177: as a reflective process, 74, 77
presence: cognitive, 14; in Community of Inquiry (CoI), 14; social, 13–14, 33, 139; teaching, 13–14, 48, 58–59, 69, 166
prior learning, 20, 23, 65, 74–79, 134, 136: assessment of, 20, 23, 65, 75, 77, 134; recognition of, 74–75
progressivism, 39
projects, 35, 48, 62, 73–75, 77, 83, 89, 95, 115–116, 120, 122, 149, 161, 163, 177. *See also* group work

quality assurance, 4, 20, 65
quizzes, 100, 114, 117–118, 175

radicalism, 40
Recognition of Prior Learning (RPL), 75–77, 89: portfolio, 78
reflection, role of, in online learning, 46. *See also* critical reflection
reflection-in-action, 44, 52
reflection-on-action, 44, 149
role-play, 95, 130, 141, 148
Rose, Ellen, 164–165
rubrics, 64, 66–68, 81–82, 140, 165

self-assessment, 8, 15, 68, 81, 86–87, 147, 149, 153–158, 161; critiques of, 156; debriefing of, 156; guided interactive, 170; how-to's, 154–155
self-reflection, 76, 156, 170–171
service learning, 61–62, 102
Shattuck, Julie, 169–170
skills gap, 6
social media, 10, 28, 98, 128, 144–146, 148: assessment of, 144–145
social software, 145–146
synchronous online learning, 32

teacher-as-facilitator, 35
teaching presence, 13–14, 48, 58–59, 69, 166
theory: of Andragogy (Malcolm Knowles), 11; of Independent Study (Charles Wedemeyer), 9–10; of Industrialization of Teaching (Otto Peters), 10; of Interaction and Communication (Börje Holmberg), 10; of Transactional Distance (Michael Moore), 9
Twitter, 98, 128, 138–139, 144, 151
types of interaction, 12

Wenger, Étienne, 12–13, 108, 157